ENTHOUS

Inspired by God

Shawn D. Sandt

ISBN 978-1-950647-23-1

Publisher's Cataloging-in-Publication data

Names: Sandt, Shawn D., author.
Title: Enthous : inspired by God / by Shawn D. Sandt.
Description: First trade paperback original edition. | Parker
[Colorado] : BookCrafters, 2019.
Identifiers: ISBN 978-1-950647-23-1
Subjects: LCSH: Faith—Fiction.
BISAC: FICTION / Religious.
Classification: LCC 3448.C48 | DDC 813 SANDT–dc22

Publishing assistance by BookCrafters, Parker, Colorado.
www.bookcrafters.net

Thirst for Knowledge

Table of Contents

Numbers
Chapter 12 Verse 6

*He said, "Listen to my words: When there is a prophet
among you, I, the Lord, reveal myself to them
in visions, I speak to them in dreams."*

NIV

Chapter 1

The Dream Is Over

April 21, 1999

4:57 a.m.

THE DREAM IS OVER. I often wake up confused and not knowing what is real life or what is just another dream. Too often, a bad dream. I repeatedly find myself thinking, did that really happen? Thinking back to the camping trip in the hills. Losing Mom and Dad had an impact on my mental state and well-being as a teenager. Little did I know back then, it would impact me for the rest of my life.

Van Halen, my favorite rock and roll band has had many great songs over the years. Of course, some more popular than others, but I probably like their entire library more than the average fan. The start to my 5:00 a.m. drive today is like so many other trips before. Once I leave the driveway, I load the album that feels right and start the music rock-in.

Ease the seat back, give everything you need, always one more, you're never satisfied, or today, hold'n faith from a string. I've never been one much to follow the lyrics, I've always been more a fan of the sound and pound. Just about any song Van

Halen plays normally helps me get from home to wherever I might be heading. Today, that would be Littleton, Colorado.

April 21st started with the alarm going off at 4:57 in the morning. By 5:05 a.m. I was headed to Colorado. Today's trip was 1,140 miles west. Littleton was going to take roughly 16 hours from my driveway in Kentucky. It was a chilly morning even though the sun was coming up. The weather in Colorado is good today, but I hear it can change in a minute. The light layer of dew covering the windshield on my Ford F-150 was gone with one swipe of the wipers. I have my typical supplies with me for the trip: a dozen peanut butter and jellies, Cheetos, a cooler of drinks, a couple apples, and my snack of choice, some Twizzlers. One loaf of bread and a few stabs at the peanut butter could make an entire weekend of meals. I've become an expert at driving across the country eating as cheaply as possible. After hugging the kids and Jennifer goodbye, I'm off again.

Leaving today is the same as always. At least the same as it's been the last couple of trips. I have promised Jennifer too many times that today would be it. No more, I was done! No more trips. No more money wasted on this sick need to find "him." No more leaving Jen and the kids to find someone who probably doesn't want to be found. Today, like many others, I'm proclaiming it to be the last. I understand and know in full what I have been risking. I can understand what her issue is, but the lack of support has become obvious throughout my last few trips. As a matter of fact, everyone in my circle of friends and family is having a problem with it. Although I haven't hurt anyone or asked for a single dime, the support is wearing off. I have invited every friend and family member along to experience the journeys with me, but in return, all I receive is a hassle.

At first, I didn't tell Jen a thing about my little secret. For over a year before I mentioned it. I wasn't trying to hide anything, I just didn't want anyone telling me their opinions. This is *my* deal. Something I'm doing for me. Something I have to do no matter the cost. Plus, I was a little nervous that she'd think I was some quack, and I truly didn't want to run her off. I would later try to convince her and everyone else in my life that my quests were going to benefit them in ways that I couldn't explain. Even if I could, they'd probably never understand.

Jen and I were at a park one night on a date when I finally did tell her. The timing seamed right. At some point, I'd have to have her approval if I was going to continue my journeys. I had mentioned early in the week that I had some big news, something important I needed to ask her. I mentioned that I had something incredible to share with her. I wanted her to be excited. That was my first mistake. Never, and I mean NEVER, say that you've got big news to pop on a date. She told everyone we knew that I was popping a different question. However, that night I told her about the accident in the mountains. I told her about everything that had happened in my life from that point on until our date that night. This was the first time that Jen would hear about my need to find "him." It was a great date and I have loved her from the minute we met, but it was that night that I finally fell in love. If I had actually had a damn ring…the night would have been perfect. I guess I'll learn one of these days.

Before I told her about my little thing in the park that night, I asked her to tell me the last time she heard of a "Jesus" spotting. We talked about what you really hear and see if you pay attention.

"If you listen and watch, it's all over the media," I told her.

Jesus spotted here, Jesus seen there. Most of those sightings are by some religious nut. As with 99% of the world, I wasn't sold, fooled, or convinced. I believe what I believe about my faith and she was on board with me. That's why I fell in love with her. That night we talked for hours about God, but also about the evils of his counterpart. Yeah, "him." It felt really good sharing that with her and having someone I could trust.

The Bible clearly says that Jesus will come back like a thief in the night. You will not know when he is coming. But where has he been? I believe that Jesus has gone to prepare us a place in the Kingdom of Heaven. Some will continue looking for Jesus. These same people probably always have and always will. That's their thing. My thing was looking for someone else: looking for him.

"Him" being the Devil, Lucifer, Satan, Abaddon, Beelzebub, the Deceiver, Leviathan, the Wicked one, or the Beast. He's the same guy. I've heard all these names from the trips I have taken. All across the country, and I'm sure all over the world, no matter what you call him he is the same asshole. He is the responsible one for so much wrong in our lives. So much death, dying, and destruction. All the good in the world is continually trumped by him. I've read that he is a former angel that fell out of favor with the Father and went the other way. We've been told that he is a beast without a care except for evil, destruction, instilling chaos, and bringing all down around him. I've always believed that "he's" a man or at least is in a man's body. We've all seen the pictures of this big monster with wings, some man looking thing with horns, a tail, and a low, deep voice that breathes fire. I've never seen a beast like this in my many travels. As a matter of fact, nobody has. But he is here. Peter, 5:8, "Be sober, be vigilant; because your adversary the devil, walks about like a roaring lion seeking whom he may devour." Oh yeah, he's up here, alright I haven't found him yet, but you can bet on this: I've seen him before and I'll find him again.

I still remember Jen's first response after I told her. She had plenty of questions. Why, where, and when again kind of things. Her face was actually the same face that everyone has when they first hear my story. That shocked look. Like you're admitting to doing something wrong. Her mouth was open, and her eyes were wide. Frozen, she couldn't say a word. Most do believe me, or they at least they say they do. Jen and everyone else know that I believe "he's" out there. I've tried to convince them all. I've seen him, talked with him, and I will catch up with him again one day. Unfortunately, today's new journey started from yesterday's tragedy. I heard it from a customer at work.

"You hear about that crap in Denver?" he asked.

"No. What crap?" I questioned.

"Guess a bunch of kids were killed this morning at some high school by a terrorist or something."

"What the...???" I was shocked.

"When?" I asked.

"About an hour ago. I think they said terrorists with guns and homemade bombs. Pretty bad deal...kids jumping out of windows and teachers being shot in classrooms. Just horrible," he said.

I was the general manager of a Mexican restaurant chain when I found that out that "he" was visiting Columbine High School in Littleton, Colorado. We didn't have a TV in the restaurant, but one of the guys had a radio in back. We turned the knob until we found a radio station with coverage. The first thing we heard was that terrorists had taken over the high school and a few dozen kids had been shot. Like most, I'm sure, my feelings were of utter shock and amazement—a blow to your stomach kind of amazement.

How does this happen in America? Nobody, including myself, knew exactly what to feel. We had the radio on that channel for the rest of the day. Everyone in the kitchen was listening intently and updating each other as to what was going on in Colorado. Although business had to continue, we all had trouble concentrating. It didn't matter that we were working over a thousand miles away, moods everywhere were the same. Shock, depression, but also frustration and anger as we looked for someone to blame.

The news anchor's voice was static and monotonous as he informed us about the deaths. "We are receiving reports of 13 students dead and many wounded by two fellow students that rampaged the classrooms with various weapons."

I exchanged a dismal glance with my staff. Everyone was in disbelief. I couldn't stop thinking about how "he" had reached those two students. The radio stopped its report and my favorite band, Van Halen came on next. A sign maybe? That immediately came to mind. Again, something as simple as a song at that exact time, gave me an urge to be there at the scene. Looking for "him."

I got home around dinner time. Jen was making the family lasagna, my favorite, as if she knew the events to come. Some people go into tough spots with fists clinched ready for a fight. A good woman like Jen went into tough spots with love, which reminds me of someone else we all know.

I entered the kitchen at home, and she asked how I was doing. Her second question was what I thought of the news from today. It was small talk about a tragedy that we had nothing to do with. We hadn't known anyone involved. Other than being compassionate fellow humans, we had nothing vested in Columbine. Our kids were in the TV room and dinner was probably ten minutes away when I told her that I had to go.

"Jen, I think I have to go to Columbine."

I just threw it out there... She knew it was coming, so why wait? I was standing across the room and she had her back to me. She stiffened her posture and then walked out of the room without even so much of a look back to me. As I said before, I had promised her that I wouldn't go on any more trips. A few minutes passed before she re-entered the room.

"When is this going to stop?" she asked.

"I don't know, Jen. Maybe never?" I replied without a definitive answer.

Before she said anything else, I continued. "I'm close, Jen, I know it. The other trips, the other people, the signs, the places, I'm getting close to him. I think even he knows it."

"Jim...you are looking for the devil! We have been over this. Everyone you know that respected you and loved you all think that you are crazy now and probably need help. I am starting to think you need help as well. If you are right, then what's the plan? Can you honestly tell me what it is that you plan on doing with 'him' if you do find him? Are you going to try kicking his ass? Yelling at him? Negotiating for mankind? Are you going to tell him to go to hell? Jim, he lives there! Why do you need to do this? Those two boys who did that terrible thing in Columbine today looked for the devil, and look what they found! Jim, don't go to Colorado," she begged.

Jen's not wrong; I've heard this for years. When we first started dating, I explained it in a way she could understand. I made it sound like I was doing something for humanity. A little something, too, for God, perhaps. I don't really know. For over the past several years, I have gone here and there searching for "him." Too many places, too many times.

Nothing was said about it for the rest of the night. She was upstairs bathing the kids and I packed up meals for the next several days. We didn't speak again for the rest of the evening. She's upset, hurt, and confused. But I know that one day it will all be worth it.

Before I left the next morning, the last thing I did was ask Jen for her forgiveness.

"Jim, I do promise you that one day I will forgive you. I do and will. But I can't promise I'll be here when you get back on Sunday. I love you, Jim!"

Well, it is what it is. My family was, and always will be, number one. However, people forget that your relationship with Jesus Christ is every bit as important, if not more so. I need to find "him" to put this all behind me, but until then? Jen, the kids, and my other family and friends will all have to deal with it.

The great Vince Lombardi once said that there are three things a man needs in life to find success: your family, your faith, and belief in the Green Bay Packers. For me, the hope in a home team is equivalent to my search for "him." And I need to win. I need to know. I know one day Jen and everyone else will understand.

The trip to Colorado ended up taking 18 hours. Most of the drive was a one lane road with miles of brown terrain and a distant, crackling lightning storm. I filtered the depressing news with some CD's all day. A lot of Van Halen. Nothing has changed. The school was obviously being searched and I had heard that bodies were still being found in the school. I've been to some rotten scenes before, but this was something I hadn't planned on.

At first, as I pulled into Denver, I noticed abandoned parking lots and an eerie quietness. There were many streets and plenty of wide, open spaces. But, as I got closer to the school, the scene changed. To say that there was a crowd at the school was an understatement. Good grief!

The traffic off the highway by the school was almost worth turning around and heading for home. It felt like I spent more time on that three mile stretch than I did the entire trip getting to Denver. It was night now and there was a glow from the school. I couldn't figure out what it was, but it looked like a field light from a sports facility during a nighttime football game. It reminded me of my own high school days as a player on the team. The Friday night lights on my face and the sound of my friends cheering was what I lived for every Friday night, but something was different about these lights. They shined like a mist from a storm cloud, and as I drove closer they illuminated the mourning faces of the people still gathered around the high school.

Alongside the school, Columbine Park rests on a small hill with groves of trees just barely hinting at bloom. The light coming from beyond the hill was fascinating in an odd way. I parked my truck and grabbed my jacket, binoculars, and a camera. The school was only 500 or so yards away, but it felt like it took me two days to reach it.

There was a movie released in the late 70's, "Close Encounters of the Third Kind." The movie was about alien aircrafts' visiting Devil's Tower in Wyoming. In the movie, the government attempted to cover it up, but the citizens knew something was going on by the dreams that they were having about it. Outside of town, people could see strange lights and nothing but military personnel coming from Devil's Tower, and the citizens had to sneak into the mountain to get a peak of what was going on behind it. Columbine felt like this to me as I was walking up past the hill, sneaking into this territory.

There wasn't any alien aircraft and there wasn't any military, but the police were ten deep in every direction. The crew in suits were the FBI, CIA, ATF, CBI, and the lights from the school were just about as bright as in that movie.

Getting a look from the hilltop to the school was a challenge. The authorities were stopping people in every direction. The more you tried walking toward the school, the tighter the security got. Driving by was out of the question. The volume of cars full of people wanting to drive by and pay their respects or say a prayer was something like I've never seen before. Thousands upon thousands of people.

When I left home that morning in Kentucky, my plan was pretty simple. Find a place to park, spend a few days looking around Columbine, and then head home that weekend. With any luck I would find "him" just along the side of the road. Or maybe in a park as people were checking out his handy work. I knew he was there, but now I had to deal with a constant flow of human traffic.

The lights were there all day and all night. However, it wasn't from a football stadium. The glow was from news trucks in every direction, every intersection, and every open space around the school. I must have counted news trucks from almost every state with blinding lighting equipment.

I went to an outdoor concert a few years back to see

Monsters of Rock. 80,000-plus people there to see Metallica, the Scorpions, Dokken, and of course the headliner, Van Halen. That crowd fired me up. Everyone was excited to be there. The energy of an outdoor concert and the mood in general is why we go, I guess.

The crowd surrounding Columbine was something else. The look alone on people's faces was exhausting. I was in Colorado for an entire day before I saw a single smile. And even that smile was tired and worn out. It had only been a day since the tragedy, but the entire community was exhausted.

I spent some time devising my strategy. I watched traffic and I watched people move to and from areas close to the school from the front seat of my truck. I had to head back to Kentucky soon and after sitting in crowds of traffic trying to get close to the school, I had only one day at Columbine. One full day of looking for "him" and that would be it. I had to find him, but I also needed to be back with my family.

I sat in my truck people-watching all night. Although most were wrapped in heavy jackets, I could make out the grief-filled looks on their faces. The crowd tapered off as the day stretched into the evening, but still hundreds, maybe thousands, of people walked from all over the city trying to get close to Columbine.

I've been people watching for years. I've been doing it for so long that I know exactly what I'm looking for, or rather whom I'm looking for. My only physical memory of "him" is from the dirt road and a few pictures. When I do find "him" though, I'll know.

The next morning, I was awake and watching. I thought I might spend a couple hours listening to the radio, but I was only 15 minutes into the news broadcast before I became too anxious. I needed to get moving. The previous day I had spotted apartments across from the school that would give me a good view to lookout for "him." About a half mile north of the school was the first entrance into the apartment complex.

Police and security officers filled every entrance. However, there was a field with tall trees and a rushing stream behind the apartments that looked like my only way in. Getting there actually turned out to be fairly easy. I walked along the street, went through the trees, and jumped a fence that led into the parking lot.

Act like you belong and nobody seems to notice. At least, that is what has worked for me during all my previous trips. I picked a southwest facing apartment and weaved my way through the sidewalks to get to the first staircase of the three-story building. I made my way to the top floor so I'd have the best view of the school. I decided that my plan was to knock on one of the apartment doors and introduce myself to the occupant. I was going to tell them that I needed a different view for a newspaper picture. I'd rather lie about why I was there than have an owner see me outside their door just to call the cops. I knocked three times on one of the heavy metal doors, but only heard an echo.

I was disappointed at first until I turned around over the balcony and realized that my viewpoint from the apartment doorway was perfect. There were other apartments that were closer to the school, but this was easy. Nobody was paying attention and I could see almost everything.

Face to face. I move from face to face with my binoculars. I'd been on the staircase for maybe an hour or so and had screened a thousand-different people. Little snap shots are all I need. There were thousands of onlookers everywhere and I could sense that officers in every direction were losing the battle of restoring peace and organization. They were trying to push water with a rake. Sooner or later, the crowds would win and surround the school entirely, flooding in and out.

I sat there people watching until about noon. Earlier I'd been worried about not getting an opportunity to get to the school, but now it looked wide open as the crowds had grown tired and

13

dispersed. It was time to make my make my way on over for a different view.

The sky was sunny, but there was a chill left in the air that made me uneasy while I walked. The media and the bulk of broadcasting were set up just in front of the school by a park. Update tents and trucks from law enforcement were set up too. The area in and around the school was busy all day, but today was a little more organized than it had been for the last day or so. If "he" is here, today would be the best day for a sighting.

Sooner or later I'm going to catch "him." I know it. I still don't have any idea what I'm going to say or do, but the man upstairs will hopefully take care of that. My instinct was telling me that "he's" here. "He's" here today.

It's the same routine as always. I spend the bulk of my time behind binoculars scanning the crowd and checking out every person in the area. When I saw "him" on the dirt road back in Kentucky "he" was dressed as a park ranger. The other times I've seen him, he was never just a guy. "He" is always up to something and always in hiding. A few years ago, I started photographing the crowds. That was Jen's idea. Little did she know that when she gave me the idea, I'd spend more time developing film than I did people watching. Oh well. Now, I never leave any site without trying to see everything and everyone and just in case I miss something, I wanted it all on film.

Then miraculously, I was watching for only ten minutes in the other direction, and I saw "him."

"Are you kidding me?" I said under my breath as I walked toward the school with my binoculars gazing from face to face.

There he was, and of all places, standing in front of the very apartment across the street where I just was. My heart felt heavy and I got chills down my back from the cool air sweeping up. As I was trying to adjust my vision and take another peak, "he" had moved toward some parked cars and got into one that

14

was pulling out. Frantically, I tried with the binoculars to get another look. Moving around the crowds around the school trying desperately to find a better view point. I'm sure it was "him," but doubt was setting in.

You have those moments in life where something freezes you. Like those unfortunate parents who received the phone call from Columbine on an ordinary Tuesday morning. For a moment I stood frozen with disbelief. The heart shuts down for just a second or two before exploding into a pounding fear, "what do I do, what does he want, why is this happening?"

I found the car in my binoculars and adjusted my vision to see "his" face. Not a doubt about it, that's "him." My previously shocked and frozen heart was now pounding like a drum. It felt like I'd been staring at him all day. He looked back at me and stood still, almost frozen himself. Is "he" really looking back at me? "He" stood there and stared back with a puzzled and confused expression which quickly melted into a spine-chilling grin. "He" knew that I had spotted him, and maybe that was his way of saying hello.

All I wanted to do was run after him. It's all I could do. I had to get to "him" before the car left. Crowds of people were still everywhere: cops on every corner, stop lights flashing, but not one thing was in my way.

"He" was now sitting in the back of an old car. Guess that was part of the show, or better yet, disguise. The car was granny smith green with a rear window bigger than most TV screens. Burning oil and smoking as it drove off. I did my best to keep my pace, but "he" and whoever was driving pulled away about 70 yards before I could get there.

I sat there, bent over trying to catch my breath, while still trying to keep an eye on the car pulling away. They were headed east, away from Columbine. The last thing I saw as the car drove off was "him" looking back through the rear-view window, through the smoke, smiling that same chilling grin.

His crooked mouth and dark eyes were almost like he was talking to me.

This time, "he" was saying see ya again soon!

John
Chapter 16 Verse 22

So, with you: Now is your time of grief,
but I will see you again and you will rejoice,
and no one will take away your joy.

NIV

Chapter 2

One Last Camping Trip

June 1984

THERE'S SOMETHING ODD ABOUT FISHING. I've often struggled, like others to sit in one spot for a long period of time for anything else. Fishing though, I could sit for hours just staring at the end of my pole waiting for something to happen. The wind blowing against the line was a joyous reason for panic.

The drive with my family that particular Saturday morning was two hours out of the city. The outlying hills of Kentucky were a nice get away with fishing streams and a beaver dam that my brothers and I loved to explore. As we arrived at the campsite for our annual camping trip, Mom was setting up supplies and Dad was tinkering with the propane tank on the RV. We had just eaten lunch and my brothers and I decided to head out. We grabbed our poles and bait box and ran excitely to the dam. I led the way through the trees and bushes while my brothers excitedly followed, tripping over stumps and uneven ground. I would stop to help them up and then continue the search for the dam.

As we reached our fishing spot, my brothers had grown tired and were bickering about who got to use the best pole, the best bait, and the best sitting spot. We hadn't been fishing for more than 30 minutes before I'd had enough. I can sit through hours of uneventful fishing, but I lost all patience when my younger brothers were wailing their high-pitched voices at each other.

"That's it, we are leaving!" I barked out.

I picked up my supplies and left. I didn't care if they followed. At first, I started walking without them, but I knew I couldn't leave them alone. I turned back, sighed, and yelled out, "Shoot, you guys have been fighting about everything. Just forget it! Let's go back."

We walked back through the woods again for about 15 minutes before reaching the dirt road opposite of our campsite. The three of us were a good 100 yards or so away from the campsite. As we rounded the corner, the last thing I remember was seeing Dad still working on the camper. I'm not sure what he was doing exactly, but Dad could fix anything. There were a series of panels where the generator, water filter, and propane tank all rested near the opened door of the camper.

Mom was standing in the doorway of the camper, smiled at us and hollered, "Hi, boys."

My brothers and I were across the road when the camper exploded. Although the second explosion was probably the deadly one, the sound of the first blast was something I'll never forget: the heat, sound, and deadly bright light. To this day, when I feel heat pressing on my skin or a blinding light, I find myself back on that dirt road again hearing my mom say, "Hi, boys."

The forest rangers said the propane tank had exploded. The initial blast probably killed my father because the tank was right above the truck's gas compartment. The second blast had taken my mother. Both were gone in seconds. The forest ranger said it was fortunate that the camper was in an opening, not close enough to the trees to start a major forest fire. Never once that day did I, or either one of my brothers, have a feeling of being fortunate. We felt isolated and sucked of all life. My brothers and I were orphaned that Saturday afternoon.

Both of my younger brothers screamed and cried in horror. I sat up on the dirt road stunned and in shock of what I had just witnessed. All three of us were knocked over backward from the blasts. They both got up and ran toward the fire with tears streaming down their faces but were forced to stop. The heat was too much even from across the road. My brothers continued to scream and collapsed to their knees. Only a few minutes had gone by when I noticed "him" walking towards us from the opposite direction.

As he approached us, I noticed his brown and green uniform. He was a park ranger, thank God. We couldn't handle any part of the hell that had just unfolded. Nothing made sense. My mind knew that my parents were gone from this moment on, but my heart wanted to believe that they were still alive.

The park ranger called to my brothers who were trying to get close to the fire, while my mother's words echoed in my ears.

"Hello, young fellas," the park ranger called out to us, oddly calm for someone walking upon such a tragedy.

He seemed less interested in the fire and more interested in the three of us. Nevertheless, he did well getting both of my brothers to sit still as we waited for more rangers and fire trucks to arrive. He looked like he was in his mid-thirties with dark, wavy hair and a tan complexion. He hadn't shaved but his uniform was well kept. He had a strange accent that I couldn't place. We were from the south, but I also knew what northerners sounded like. It wasn't a western accent either.

"Sir, where are you from?" I asked after he got control of the scene and helped me and my brothers up.

"A guess perhaps," he said with a sly grin.

"Europe? Maybe Australia?" I asked.

With a grunt and a sigh, he replied, "No, somewhere in the middle." And that was the end of that.

The camper had burned itself out almost completely before the other rangers and fire trucks arrived. What was once our truck, our family's camper, and our two parents was now a faltering flame and a heap of metal. I was terrified to look at the scene in fear of seeing the remains of my parents. As we sat there, the emotions of the event started to hit us all. Some of the rangers wept with us, but it hit me the hardest when I realized I was going home that night without my parents, forever. My little brothers and I would cry not only that day but for months and years to come.

Time didn't matter that afternoon. We sat close to our parents for the last time. By then, more rangers and nearby campers had arrived and offered assistance. Everything was gone except for three boys, three fishing poles, and my dad's tackle box. I knew right then and there I'd have that tackle box with me forever.

One of the nearby camping families had noticed smoke over the mountain top and they came to check things out. They had some kids with them, one of which was my age. As the day was becoming night, they asked to take us home until my grandparents could be reached and informed of the tragedy. I wanted to say goodbye and thank you to the first ranger who had helped us, but he was nowhere to be found. He disappeared around the same time the other park rangers arrived. We never noticed him leave. It would become part of the accident investigation for weeks, months, and years later. I had to repeat my story to all kinds of law agencies about who that first ranger was. We never got a name. All I could tell the investigators was what he was wearing, how he looked, and about his strange accent. Over the next two years I was asked over and over again if I knew who he was, but I knew nothing.

He seemed like a nice guy that just happened to walk up on a bad accident. One day, about a year after the accident, an ATF agent asked questions about the fire. This was one of many interviews about that accident. They tried wrapping up the case for quite some time, but oddly, the park ranger who first approached us from "somewhere in the middle" was not on any payroll and didn't match a single description of park rangers in that area. If it had just been me telling the story, they might have thought I dreamt about him. But try as they might, together as a group my brothers and I had the same story down to the smallest details.

That day, we left with the camping family who had come to help us. The Gurmendi's, from Peru. It worked out that they lived just a few miles from our parents' house. They were what appeared to be a great family. I hadn't known anyone from Peru until I met them. One of the sons, Aldo, was the craziest kid I had ever met. He would later turn out to be the guy that got me into more trouble in high school than I could have possibly planned for myself. Although we were always breaking the rules, he brought me more tears of laughter than any person had in my life. He became one of my very best friends.

Sunday morning, after the accident, Mrs. Gurmendi made breakfast and all ten of us went to church.

Are you kidding me? I thought.

My parents and grandparents were all church-going, God-fearing people, but it was less than 24 hours after the accident I was just mentally and physically drained. I would really have like to watch some mind-numbing TV in a dark room all day. I didn't complain (verbally) and neither did my brothers. So all ten of us piled into their station wagon and went to church.

While I sat there in the pew that day, swatting the fly that was buzzing around my head, I heard the pastor say, "Death is not the end of the story for those who know the Lord."

He went on to explain that while the afterlife is of glory with God, we must first go through judgment for what we have done in our lives, whether good or bad.

At that point the blood started to rush through my body, and my face felt hot. Why did such a bad thing happen to my parents when they were so good and always went to church? What did they do to deserve this? And if God is so good then why did this awful thing have to happen? I couldn't understand why my parents were taken from me. What did I do to deserve that? Who is doing this to me?

I wouldn't be able to tell people what I was actually feeling for years. Hell, it still confuses me. I also couldn't tell anyone how I felt, not only being the oldest brother, but now the oldest member of my family and along with it the newfound grave responsibility I would have for my brothers.

"Why, God?" was all I could ask.

1 Peter
Chapter 5 Verse 8

Be alert and of sober mind.
Your enemy the devil prowls around like a
roaring lion looking for someone to devour.

NIV

Chapter 3

World War II

February 1988

IT'S BEEN ALMOST FOUR YEARS since losing my parents. The first year was the toughest, but the following years were a blur. I was looking forward to prom, parties, and being done with high school. Graduation day was right around the corner. I got my driver's license, played sports, hung out with friends, and argued with my grandparents about any and everything. I was a pretty typical teenager and I'm not sure if having my parents alive would have changed much.

My grandfather was a truck driver, and my grandmother was a semi-retired sales manager at a funeral home. They both had to scale back the number of hours they worked after becoming full time parents again. My grandmother took things pretty seriously. She was always on my brothers and me for something: making beds, brushing teeth, homework, and always going to church. Having three young boys in the house was stressful for her after having raised two well-behaved daughters. My grandfather, on the other hand, loved having us around to throw baseballs with, watch football games, and fish together. He had married and had his daughters right after leaving the Navy, so my grandfather finally received some much-needed male bonding from my brothers and me.

Little did I know, the moment my brothers and I sat on the couch, flipping through my grandfather's picture albums, would forever change my life. My grandfather sat in the middle of the couch with my brothers nestled under each arm. All three of them turning page after page of the photo album: laughing, questioning, and storytelling. Most of them were black and white pictures and every one of them had a story.

That particular morning on the couch, my brothers were asking questions about the photos. The great thing about pictures is they all have a story. I sat there listening from across the room and imagined myself in the scenes that Gramps was describing. The three of us sat silently when he spoke about his days in World War II. Not just that morning, but anytime WWII came up.

Gramps served in the Navy for four years after dropping out of high school. He was good at what he did. Deck Master: the sailor at the helm, or in short, the guy who drives the boat. It took him some time, but after going through the ranks he found himself at the helm of some of the grandest ships in the Navy.

While flipping from page to page, he told us that back then, things across the globe were unraveling. War was breaking out everywhere. But what was my grandfather doing? Breaking out cigars to celebrate his newborn child. His first, and my mom's older sister.

He was stationed in Honolulu, Hawaii serving on the US Arizona in Pearl Harbor and went on leave December 5, 1941 for the birth of my aunt. The horrible day in Hawaii was on December 7th. You never know how things will turn out, but who knows, if he had been there that day, my grandparents may have never had a second child; my mother.

After my aunt was born, my grandfather couldn't wait to get back into the action. He felt as if he had let his country down by not being in Pearl Harbor on that day. President Roosevelt told the country that we were now at war. For my grandfather who had just lost so many friends, so many brothers, getting back to the Navy was all he wanted to do.

He explained to us how back then the paperwork process in the Navy wasn't what it is today. Records weren't exactly the sharpest. Long before emails and fax, your paperwork or "orders" were issued on a receipt. Carbon copy pieces of paper with instructions on where to report. That, and a bus pass, were just about all you received. Gramps joked that the paperwork process was so bad, that at times a sailor could receive orders, report for duty, fight in part of a war, die, and get shipped home in a body bag before the paperwork reached the shipyard announcing his expected arrival date.

Gramps was on a bus heading for San Francisco right before Christmas. All he showed up with was his transfer paperwork, a copy of his driver's license, proof of his authorized leave, and military issued dog tags. The only clothes he had were on his back.

"What's your job boy?" A large, intimidating man with uniform and a buzz cut had asked my grandfather.

"I'm a Deck Master on the Arizona in Pearl," he had responded back eagerly.

"Well son, just this morning we got news that a better portion of the fleet in Pearl is gone. What do you want to do?" the station officer would ask my grandfather.

"I'll do whatever you need me to do. I just want to make a difference. Send me where you want, I'll do what I'm asked," my grandfather replied.

Back then, America was a little different. My grandfather didn't have a change of clothes and or any real proof of who he was and where he was going. He was like many American men back then: eager and willing to make a difference. After less than an hour spent with the port officer, he was headed to join up with the USS Indianapolis, another one of America's great war ships. It wasn't long either, late February in 1942, until he would be back in the waters of the South Pacific. He was on the Indianapolis for over three years.

My brothers and I asked all types of questions about his next few years spent in the South Pacific. "How many ships did y'all sink? Did you ever have Kamikazes hit you? How many islands did you visit? Or see? Or bomb?"

Grandpa would shake his head and say that there was too much hell to talk about that time of his life. The only stories that we ever heard were told that morning. For a guy who talked and told as many stories as Gramps did, it was weird to us that he never spoke much about his naval experience.

He did tell us that that summer was hot, and the war was going on in full swing. One morning in particular, a rumor began on deck spreading from ship to ship. The supply ships that carried fuel, ammunition, letters from home, and food had been attacked and sunk the day before. Immediately, the brass went into wartime rationing. Every bullet, every gallon of gasoline, and every green bean was accounted for. Although they would not see supplies again for over two weeks, they carried on business as usual to give the Japanese an image of domination, rather than the vulnerable situation at hand. As the days went on, food become a concern. It was 16 days before they received supplies. Gramps told us that each man on each ship ate only green beans for each meal. It was green beas for breakfast, lunch, and dinner for the last three days until they were finally restocked. The last day, prior to receiving supplies, each man only received four green beans for each meal that day.

The term, "war was hell," was used often that morning. Gramps spoke of few things prior to discussing the morning of July 30, 1945. His voice and his entire mood, demeanor changed as he spoke about that event. He said, "Just after midnight, the Indianapolis was struck by two torpedoes on her starboard bow, from a Japanese submarine. A complete surprise with explosions that caused massive damage. Twelve minutes later the ship had rolled over completely, the stern rose up into the air, and down it plunged. About 300 men on board died immediately. The rest of the crew, 880 men plus or minus, all went overboard. Few made it to lifeboats, and many without lifejackets floated in the water awaiting rescue.

Gramps told us he was off duty and asleep at the time. Just a few minutes after midnight he found himself on the floor, still asleep in everything but his boots. It was that sudden. After the first torpedo hit, the clear-all alarm sounded and a race to find moonlight was in full swing. Panic and chaos were everywhere. He did grab a life jacket and made it overboard before the ship sank.

The fact that he, and 880 others, fought for three days to stay alive in the open water was a terrifying thought. What all those men had to endure for three days after the Indianapolis was below the water? Not having food or water was probably a little rough. Floating in the open water for the sun to beat you up non-stop, hour after hour must have been horrible. Floating in the open water waiting for the sharks. I can't even think of it.

My little brother did ask, "Gramps, what was the worst part?"

He shook his head side to side and went pale. "You can't even imagine," was all Gramps would say.

Only 300, give or take, made it out of those waters alive. Only 300. For a young boy, that was a cool story. Probably my favorite of all of Gramps' stories. A sad, tragic, but completely true story right from our very couch. The same couch where the next picture we saw would tell of a completely different narrative.

Sitting there arm to arm as my grandfather continued turning the pages of his photo album, he stopped briefly and pointed something out. It was a picture with some of his shipmates sometime before the sinking, in the Tinian Island. The picture had about a dozen guys in it.

Gramps pointed to a few different guys in that picture and mentioned their names. He still remembered. He mentioned what they had done on the ship, and also if they made it out alive. Most of the guys in that picture had not.

My youngest brother pointed to one man and asked, "Who's this?"

"Not sure, really. Don't remember his name. I'm not sure what he even did on the ship. Heck, all I remember is that was the fella with a weird accent," he replied.

It was just a sailor whose name my grandfather couldn't recall. What he would recall was that he had a strange accent that Gramps said he couldn't place. He told us that he had asked him where he was from one day. The unknown sailor asked if my grandfather had any guesses.

"Europe? Maybe Australia?" Gramps had asked him.

"Nope, somewhere in the middle," is all that the unknown sailor replied.

Immediately I felt a familiar chill run through my spine.

"What did you just say?" I demanded with a harsh tone in my voice. Before that, I hadn't uttered a word all morning.

With a stunned look on his face as I barked out those words, my grandfather repeated, "somewhere in the middle."

Before I could get out of my chair, my youngest brother said, "Isn't that the park ranger that disappeared?"

I quickly moved over to the couch and sat beside the three of them and stared for a moment without uttering a word. It only took a quick glance to locate "him" in the picture, but after I found him, I knew it. It was the park ranger.

"Impossible!" was all I could say.

My other brother also agreed. Although it was black and white, it was as clear as any colored picture. His eyes, his build, and his wavy hair were all the same as the guy dressed as the park ranger on the dirt road a few years ago.

"Him?" My grandfather pointed and asked. His face was puzzled. "Are you three boys trying to tell me that is the guy who helped you a few years ago after the accident? That he's the same guy who disappeared and the police have been looking for?"

"Yes, Gramps...that's him," said all three of us while nodding our heads up and down.

"Gramps. He even answered your question the same way the park ranger answered mine. 'Somewhere in the middle.' The same answer to the question we both asked him. How does that happen?"

The four of us sat looking at the picture for the rest of the morning. As hard as we tried, Gramps wouldn't buy it. Every time I tried to convince myself he was just a look-alike, it didn't work. I knew that the man in the picture was the same man as the park ranger.

That day of storytelling would be the first day of a journey I'd be on for who knows how long. After seeing *that* picture of *that* sailor, I knew that he and the park ranger were the same guy. I wasn't sure how, but I knew it in my heart.

Around lunch we finally put the photo albums away and Gramps uttered some final words. "Well kids, that's probably a guy who looks very much like the park ranger, but he was my age back in the 40s. That's 40 some odd years ago. There's just no way he's the same fella."

"Gramps...you're wrong. That's him, and I'm pretty sure I know exactly who that is too." I said.

"Well, who do you think it is, Jimmy?"

"Gramps....that's the devil!"

Matthew 25 Verse 40

The King will reply,
"Truly I tell you, whatever you did for
one of the least of these brothers and sisters
of mine, you did for me."

NIV

Chapter 4

The King with Everything

April 1990

ONE MORNING IN THE LATE SPRING OF 1990, my grandmother called and asked me how college was going. I was in school studying psychology. I thought it might be great to use my mind to open the minds of others, or something like that. I had started in a business program the previous year and instead of psychology was thinking about changing again to something in sports, perhaps. To tell you the truth, I really didn't even know. It was looking like the typical four-year plan might turn into five or six years.

Now don't get me wrong, I was having a blast. My freshman year in the dorms could have been a television series. The day to day drama and lifestyle was something better left unspoken. The fact that my grandparents were paying for it was embarrassing. It was a smaller state school specializing in education and music. They also had a good business school. Me? I was specializing in nothing of the sort.

Grandma had called just about every week since I left for college. The usual call was just the pleasantries. How are the classes? How are my new friends? Even though she would ask about activities, she had heard stories about my freshman year and so she didn't ask what she didn't want to hear. However, this particular day, something else was on her mind.

My grandfather was an operator of a tractor trailer owned by a grocery chain. He had worked for years full-time as a truck driver, but since becoming a full-time father again, his workload had to decrease. He needed the money, but with three young boys around, driving 40 hours a week wasn't an option.

After just a brief minute of speaking on the phone, she made the statement, "Jimmy...your granddad has been hurt."

It was nothing too serious, but he had a broken arm. He had fallen off the loading ramp at one of his stops. She said the ice was built up around the cement deck and his hand was in his pocket so he could not pull it out in time to brace himself for the six-foot fall. His entire body had crashed against his trapped arm on his side. He was lucky it was only his arm.

I had been at college just short of two years. Or rather, I'd been away at a party for two years. Even though I had a couple weeks left of my sophomore year, once I got that call, I was done. I was doing nothing worthwhile in college anyway. I packed and left the next morning.

My grandfather needed surgery. He was transported to a local hospital in some small town where he was dropping off his load. All they did was stabilize his arm for the trip home. I spoke with Grandma and told her I would love to go get him. From where I was to where he was, it would take about 10 hours to make the round trip.

Heading off in his direction, I spent a good part of the morning thinking of Mom and Dad. I missed them both, but I missed my dad a great deal. Not a day goes by where I don't think of him. Of course, my dad was younger and had the energy for doing anything with his three sons. Although my grandfather didn't have the same energy when he moved into the full-time dad role again, never once did I feel like I was missing out on anything. I have been blessed to have him.

Since leaving for college, I hadn't seen Gramps very much. Actually, thinking back, I had done a pretty crappy job of keeping in touch. I was reminded one day, not too long ago, that I hadn't been fishing with Gramps since leaving for college. Going to get him wasn't just what he needed, but also was what I needed.

After I got him outside the clinic's door, his emotions were running high. He had to be drugged up pretty well for the pain. The nurse and I got him buckled in the car and off we went. Thanks to the pain killers I heard, "I love you," about twice a minute for the duration of the drive.

For the first hour Gramps was in and out. One minute he was snoring so loud you might have thought there was a leaf blower on in the car. The next minute he was awake rambling on about family, love, kids, death, God and fishing. All kinds of endless chatter. He went on and on, bouncing around from one subject to another. Right about then I was praying for an actual leaf blower to drown him out.

Soon after, he drifted off for quite a while. I probably had the radio on a little louder than I normally would have. In the countryside there were only a few stations and a lot of them were hillbilly radio. I was just about ready to give up finding something I liked when, oddly enough, I ran across "Right Now," a classic off my favorite Van Halen album.

Again the lyrics are great, but the sound is something that worked well to keep me alert and awake. A couple things I heard loud and clear. Make future plans, don't waste time dreaming about yesterday, says a lot to me. "Catch a magic or special moment and do it right here and now," says even more.

Roughly 90 miles outside of home, I looked over and noticed Gramps was wide awake. He had been out for over an hour and was just sitting there like he was fighting off a hangover. I wasn't sure what to do or say, but right here and now was a perfect time to maybe catch a magic moment.

"How you feeling Gramps? Would you like me to pull over and let you out so you can jog home?" I asked with a wink and a sly grin.

A little groggily he replied, "Nah. Actually we probably need the gas money. Just pull over and shut the engine off. I'll just push us home!"

We both eye-balled one another and had a good chuckle. I had just spent two years with nothing but smart asses trying to be comedians, but not a single guy in college was even close. Gramps was truly the best.

Immediately he asked, "I noticed in the back that there are a lot of bags and boxes?"

He had been paying for the majority of my school for the past two years although he himself had never made it out of the eighth grade. A grandson in college? At one time he was the proudest man around. He, having not even graduated high school, and now his grandson was off to get a college diploma? Oh, this might be a tougher trip than I had planned.

"Yep..." I said hesitantly and sat there for a minute before continuing.

"Gramps, I'm not going back. I'm sorry, but I'm not doing what I should be doing. I can't explain it in a way that you might understand. I really feel like I'm supposed to be doing something else. I'm not sure exactly what though, but I know I won't find it in a textbook or a classroom."

A minute went by before either of us would continue.

"Remember the story I told you about the birth of your aunt? I was off on leave from the Navy and had just become a dad for the first time? Do you remember what happened to me on December 7th?

"Pearl Harbor," I said.

"Ahh...no! What happened to me? I said!" He would reply.

"I told my wife, your grandmother, that I just couldn't explain it. Couldn't explain it to her in a fashion that she'd understand. I told her I felt like I was supposed to be doing something else. Not exactly sure what though, but something else. She argued that I could find a job here or go back to school. Now that was funny. I told her that not only was I going back to the Navy, but I was going as soon as they'd let me!

"Junior, I can almost guarantee that I might be the *only* person who understands *exactly* how you're feeling. Probably a little lost and unsure of what the future may hold for you? Are you feeling empty and short on emotions, short on finances, and short on your spirit, too?"

Nodding my head yes and reaching toward the radio dial to turn the volume down, I replied, "Yes, that would be me."

"Did I ever tell you the story about The King with Everything?"

"Nope, I don't recall ever hearing it," I said.

My grandfather is the best storyteller of all time. The mood, situation, need, it made no difference. He always had something awesome. I've heard more stories about places, people, and things than any other man alive. At least that I know of.

This story was a good one. Gramps started to tell of a long time ago about this King with Everything. Apparently, he had it all. God had gold, silver, and jewels like no other. He had not only the best of paintings and sculptures, but the artists worked right there in The King's castle. He had his family dressed in the best of linens with all of them custom made. His castle was built by the finest architects and laborers you could employ. His military was big and powerful, they were like no other. He was of perfect health and his body was like the saying, a Greek god! He and his family ate fine meals every day and he was educated by the finest schools from the time of his birth. And finally, the women. There wasn't a woman from coast to coast who wouldn't fall to his feet from even the slightest hint of a smile from him. He was The King with Everything.

One day late in his life, this King had one of his many sons ask him... "Father, when you die, how would you like those in your Kingdom to remember you?"

This question from his young son troubled The King. Even though this King lived well and better than any, he tried to be a great man for all of those within The Kingdom. He wasn't an evil man or a bad man. He always liked the idea of doing something good. He always tried to show love, care, and even mercy for his people when needed. He wasn't a push over, but even in tough times he was fair to all. What would the people of his Kingdom say about him after he was gone? That question troubled The King.

He would say, "Son, I'm not sure how my people would answer that question today. I apologize for not being better prepared for you and your curiosity, but come again tomorrow and you may find an answer!" His son left smiling.

Well, the next day The King would rise from bed with a different agenda than usual. With passion and vigor, The King ordered his knights of the round table to go without fear to the farthest edges of The Kingdom and collect his people. Not just any people, but to collect the experts from every field of science, religion, medicine, philosophy, sports, history, military, and on, and on, and on. His only commandment to his knights was that they collect the experts in every field of study known.

Months later, in the grand ballroom of The King's castle stood thousands of people. All of which specialized in their trade. Men and women, young and old, it didn't matter. Each of them experts in their professions. Many of which had never seen the castle, not to mention The King. His guest eagerly waited, not only to possibly meet The King, but also to serve in any way they could.

Before he entered the room, he had them fed. All the guests ate and drank like Kings themselves. He had gifts and entertainment for the experts. The King's best clowns and comedians brought them to laughter, and he had the highest priest tell stories of Jesus that gave hope to all. It wasn't until late day that The King with Everything would make his presence to his guests.

An eerie silence grew as the guests stood before The King. Not a word or a sound was heard. Guests in the back could hear as easily as those closest to him. Not a person in the room, even his closest family and friends, knew of what was about to come.

"My family, my friends, my people. I owe everything to you. My life, I owe to you. Thank you. Everything in our Kingdom is because of you. For that, I bring you here today to give you a taste of life only a King would know. I hope you have enjoyed the food and gifts. There is more of that to come. For the task that I am about to present to you, I promise you and your families that each and every day for the rest of your lives will be the same as today."

Now, this King needed these people. Little did anyone know that he wanted a task completed before he passed. The task was simple. He would continue with simple instruction and ask for nothing but the best from them. He made it very clear that anything less than perfection would be dealt with harshly. As he continued, many asked questions, but after just a short time, each knew exactly what was expected. Each had to write out and explain his or her field of expertise in a fashion for all to read and understand.

These writings would be complied into a series of books, not only for The King to read and enjoy, but so that anyone who wanted to understand could have access to the material. The first encyclopedia set of mankind.

The King gave them one year to complete the task. After more questions, the group quickly came up with a plan and promised The King that he would see them all this same day, exactly one year from now. Off they went.

True to the group's word, they did return. They returned with books. Lots and lots of books. Each and every one of those books with hundreds of pages. Many of those pages with hand drawn pictures. Many other pages with written proofs for math and science problems. There were maps, poems, stories, and endless information about anything the reader, or in this case, The King, would ever want to know.

The King was in shock. What was completed and submitted to him was beyond his original hopes and expectations. The more he read, the more amazed he was. There was one problem though. The amount of information was too much. He was gifted with tens of thousands of pages in these books. Although, this is exactly what he had requested, he had yet another task for the same group.

The King requested that the same information be rewritten and fit into a single book. He made it very clear that all would benefit from the completion of this new task in the same way that they would all be punished for failing. He needed this one book returned and completed in one month's time.

There were more questions, complaints, and grumbling by many. But nevertheless, what The King wanted, he received. So off they went on their new task.

As expected, the group returned with the completed book. All the information was now condensed to a single book of several hundred pages. The King was so delighted that he cried while reading through his new book. The crowd knew by the expression on The King's face as he read through it, that it was not only completed, but completed well. Or, so they thought.

"My people, the book that you have all worked on is almost perfect," The King started to say.

He continued about an idea to have something for every man, woman and child in his Kingdom to have to help better their lives. Each and every citizen regardless of age, race, and color could have a gift from The King that they could in-turn use to better their own lives. What the King needed from the group was the same information communicated and written down on a single page. The King demanded it to be completed in only one week.

The group returned in six days, excited to finally have it done. Each and every group member was confident that The King would enjoy and appreciate the single page of information from what was once thousands of pages of information. To their surprise, The King had one final request.

The King began, "My loyal and most trusted people. Thank you is not enough. Gifts of gold and wealth could not repay what you have done for me. I truly am in your debt. However, I have one final request. This new single page? By this time tomorrow, I need this even smaller. Yes, I need all the information that has been gathered from all of you and I need it in one single sentence. Good luck and I'll see you tomorrow."

The group was beyond amazed. These men and women from all over The Kingdom had been working on this task for well over a year. Each of them impressed that, not only did they got everything written down in a series of books to begin with, but that they more impressively broke all that information down to a single book, and then to a single page. Now they were being asked to provide a single sentence?

Once again, the group did not disappoint. By lunch of the next day, The King had his sentence. One single, well written sentence that The King could give to all his people for generations to come. This single sentence would carry across the globe for the rest of time. All the experts from each field carefully chose the correct words, gave the correct input to what each man, woman, and child would need not only to have a chance, but to improve on whatever it was The King might see. This single sentence gifted from a King for all those who would read it.

I sat there and continued to drive with my eyes on the road and my attention on Gramps. For a second, I was expecting him to continue the story with The King wanting a single word, but

Gramps ended the story and didn't continue. I looked over at him briefly and caught a little grin. He was waiting for me to ask it...

"Well, what the hell was the sentence?" I asked with both irritation and excitement.

"I can't remember," Gramps shook his head as if he was confused, but I suspected it was an act. This was one of his endless opportunities to have fun at my expense.

"If I have to stop this car...I swear to God!" I said as if I was upset, but we both knew better.

"That last task was to complete that single sentence. That sentence was The King's one and only message for his people. A gift for all, including us today." Gramps again looked at me briefly with a serious face.

"Junior, The King's message was simple. 'There is no such thing as a free lunch!'"

Jeremiah
Chapter 29 Verse 11

For I know the plans I have for you,"
declares the Lord, "Plans to prosper you
and not to harm you, plans to give
you hope and a future.

NIV

Chapter 5

Any Plan Will Do

THERE'S NO SUCH THING AS A FREE LUNCH. I repeated that sentence in my head off and on the rest of the drive home. That was good. I'll remember that one for a while, maybe forever. It was typical Gramps too, one of his many long-winded stories about something that hopefully his grandson could reflect on and do something about. Both he and Grandma had all kinds of stories. The art of their tale telling was that you never knew if it was fact or fiction. But each and every story would inspire to change or influence one of their grandchildren in a positive way.

We spoke about many things on that drive back home. My brothers, Grandma, even my parents. We spoke a tad about his time in World War II and of my college for a bit. More specifically, we spoke about what kind of beer his money had bought at my college. Every time school came up, I did everything I could to change the subject. Our longest talk was about his own career. Only then I could ditch the college chatter. What a waste of time for me, that it had been.

Since becoming a full-time parent again, he worked many jobs to be able to support our family. At one point earlier in his life, he worked the oil fields in Texas and Oklahoma. They called it rough necking. He spent all day out in the hot sun or cold winter lugging 200-pound pipes in ankle deep mud. And those were the easy days. Working in the fields sounded like hell. Just hearing him go on about the manual labor and hours needed in his "oil days" guaranteed one thing: I would never work that industry, never a single day.

How he got into trucking was yet another one of Gramps' stories. He went on about leaving work and heading home one day. A normal summer day, he called it. A mile or two outside the job site, along some roadway in the back country, he came upon a rig, an 18-wheeler, that was off on the side of the road with some kind of trouble. Now Gramps never passed someone on the side of the road without trying to help. By the time I was born, Grandma told me that Gramps had changed more tires than the service station down the street. It was just in his nature to help.

He continued to tell me that the old man driving the rig had some engine issues. He didn't tell me much about what was wrong with the engine, but Gramps said he had it working again in no time. He also said that just a few minutes with that old man wound up changing his life forever.

That old man, Fred Wright was his name, owned a trucking company. He had that rig, a trailer, and a few more like it. The rig he was working on that day when my grandfather pulled up was an old Kenworth 100 series cab over a semi-truck. It wasn't fancy like the rigs today with beds, TV's, and kitchens in them. However, the Kenworth was strong. Gramps said it could pull just about anything as fast as he wanted to drive it.

Apparently, Fred Wright was quite a storyteller as well. To say they hit it off immediately is an understatement. Gramps talked about more things than any man I have ever met, but he told me that he couldn't get a word in that day. They had the rig fired up in 15 minutes and then they sat there chatting for another two hours. The old man, Fred, was nearing the end of his career. He was too old to run beets and wheat all over the south and needed a way out. Gramps needed a way in. He was just starting life with a new wife and a couple young girls. He didn't have an extra dime in his pocket, but by the following Monday morning he was the co-owner of a trucking company.

They had made a handshake deal right there on the side of the road. Fred was going to retire and take payments. He had nothing else to retire on. His trucking company was it, but he couldn't put forth the energy and effort anymore to make it work. My grandfather, true to his word, made payments until Fred's death. They had a monthly percentage deal. Gramps could grow the business, shrink it, and haul whatever his heart desired. From that handshake on the side of the road Fred collected a check every month for 17 years and not once was ink put to paper.

About 20 minutes from home Gramps asked, "So what's your plan now?"

"What plan?" I replied.

"Well, if you are not going back to school, do you have a plan? For work?"

"I hate to say this Gramps, but I don't. I don't have a clue about what I'm going to do."

Gramps asked a question that he probably already knew the answer to. He offered to make calls to different guys he knew from different industries. We even spoke about a career in the military. However, I was truly lost on the subject.

Gramps threw out one more suggestion, "Jim, find a plan and go with it. Sometimes, any plan will do!"

He continued off in another direction. "What about a lady? Do you have a regular squeeze?"

Laughing, I looked in his direction and asked... "Maybe we could talk about a job instead!"

We both chuckled.

"Actually I do have my heart on this girl. Her name is Jennifer and her family is an hour or so from home. She is studying biology... or science, or nursing, or something. Hell, I actually don't even know. All I know is that she is great. Looks darn good too."

"You been dating her long?" Gramps asked.

"Yeah, on and off for about 11 months. She was slowly getting away from this dead-beat boyfriend she's had for a few years. She told me that she would rather not jump right into another relationship so there is an odd distance at times between us."

After a brief silence I continued... "There is a new development between us," as I smiled at him.

"Does she know about your folks?"

"Yeah she does. She also knows about you, Grandma, the whole family."

"Well that's good. So, do you think she likes you?" he asked.

"I do. But like I said, she is keeping a little distance, figuring things out in her own life."

"Well Jr, sounds like BS to me. She is not telling you the whole story about something," he proclaimed. He always spoke his mind. He was normally all too accurate with his feelings too.

There are two guarantees about southerners. Number one, most don't hold their tongue and they will tell you exactly what is on their mind, never mind anyone's feelings. Honesty and the brutal truth are the only ways many southerners speak. The other guarantee is that I seem to run into more people, my grandparents included, that are able to sniff out the truth. I've lied a time or two to my grandparents and never once was successful. That old man Fred probably knew my grandfather was as honest a man from that first-hand shake. Well, right now, Gramps is dead on, again. Not about Jennifer, but about something else.

"Gramps, it's me not telling you the whole story," I said sheepishly.

"Oh, really?"

"Yeah, she and I get along well. Real well. Probably too well. Our backgrounds, our families, friends, heck, even our personal issues complement each other. But there's an issue that she's trying to get her hands around."

After what seemed like forever, Gramps asked… "And that would be?"

Not really knowing how to say it, I stuttered, "Gramps, it's something about me. I probably need to tell you about it and get your opinion. I might like your thoughts on the matter. I don't think Jen understands it and she might be struggling on how to accept this deal."

Just about then, we pulled into the neighborhood. The conversation for the past several hours had been great. I think, although in pain, Gramps enjoyed it as well. This was going to be a tough one. Not only was the issue odd, but we are literally out of road as the driveway is just down the street and this conversation could be hours in the making.

As I pulled into the driveway, Gramps looked at me and said, "What kind of deal, Jimmy? You in trouble?"

"Nope, not yet. Maybe not ever, either. Jen and I have told each other all kinds of things. Heck, darn near everything. Jen knows all about that horrible day in the hills. She even knows about you. I told her all about your time in the Navy. I've told her just about everything."

"And?" Gramps asked with anticipation.

"Well, I told her without a doubt I am 100% positive that the devil is alive and well working his BS around and amongst us all. She asked if it was true, and what I was going to do about it."

Gramps sat there with this look of shock and confusion on his face, "And?" He said.

"Well, like I told you earlier. I don't know what I'm doing tomorrow much less what I would do about the devil right now. But mark my words, I'm going to find his ass and deal with him then!" I told him excitedly.

48

"Jimmy, help me get inside. Let's get settled and then we need to talk."

John
Chapter 5 Verse 19

Very truly I tell you, the son can do nothing by himself; he can only do only what he sees his father doing, because whatever the father does, the son also does.

NIV

Chapter 6

Supper Club

Summer 1992

OUR SON WAS BORN IN THE SPRING OF 1992. Although we hadn't planned on having a child before being married, I believe that God's greatest gifts come on his schedule, not ours.

Also, that spring, Gramps finally re-retired from work. He couldn't handle it anymore after his injury a few years prior. He was approaching 70, and trucking isn't the sit on your butt and chat on the CB radio all night long like some may think. Often, he had to help unload and work docks to get the load rolling. Physical work that he just couldn't handle anymore.

Immediately after Gramps' accident, I was directionless. I had dropped out of school, had no job, and other than my immediate family, I had nothing stable. About a week after getting Gramps home following the first surgery on his arm, he received a phone call. Fred needed some help, and my grandparents needed some money. Unfortunately, Gramps was in no condition to drive, but his oldest grandson was.

It was on the job training starting from day one. I'd been in a few of Gramps' rigs way back when, but never behind the wheel. My training was on the go and the trainer was riding right beside me. Gramps was with me from the very start.

Driving a truck isn't a bad living. If you like seeing the countryside, then it's the perfect line of work. Some like the isolation or freedom away from typical "co-workers." It took me ten, maybe 15 long runs before I got the hang of it, and once I did I gave it some consideration as a career. Then, of course, came my first semi-truck tire change. No way in hell was I going to do this forever. About a week later, Gramps re-retired and I quit the trucking business.

That summer was full of events. The main event was of course, my wedding. Jen's parents, being very traditional people, took care of most of the wedding costs. At one point during the planning, they offered us a lump of money in lieu of a typical church and reception styled wedding. Did we really need all the bridesmaids, limos, and cocktail bars? They had suggested we take the money and run. Maybe a midnight run to Las Vegas? That might only cost a couple hundred bucks and the rest we could pocket. We skipped the cash offer and went with planning and having a wedding Jen had dreamed about.

Sometime in early April, Jen and I were out searching for a reception hall. It was a Saturday morning and we had scheduled visits with a few properties. The banquet manager at one hotel was an older lady named Ona Mae. She'd been in the business for years and she was working at a standard hotel with a ballroom. She would tell us during our first visit that she had seen and planned more weddings than a Las Vegas drive through chapel. She was charming, funny, and seemed very honest. Jen and I liked her immediately.

Long before that visit with Ona Mae, several years ago when Jen and I first started dating, I told Jen about "him." She knew all about my belief that the devil was amongst us and was up to no good, wrecking lives, and destroying anything he could. She knew about my parents and that terrible day in the mountains. She knew about that park ranger, too. She also knew all about my grandfather. In fact, she never knew her grandfather and warmed up to mine the minute they met. It was fair to say, she knew me and my background as well as, if not better, than any other person in my life.

When we arrived that Saturday, Ona Mae walked us around the entire hotel. The property had about 200 rooms in the four-story building. Although the property was pretty old, the ballroom where wedding receptions took place was simple, classy, and complete. We could get in, do our thing, and get out. Everything was easy and going well with our visit. We could have been in and gone with a deal wrapped up, but then of course, Jen asked Ona Mae one particular question.

"So what was the craziest day in all your years in this business?"

Ona Mae replied, "Oh, that's simple. It was both the craziest and worst day of my life. Back in late spring of '77 I think." She sat there and looked at us staring back at her.

As we waited, we were halfway expecting to hear her answer Jen's question about some crappy day with the weather or maybe how some limo driver lost a bride. But no, her answer was something else. You could tell by the look on her face, Ona Mae was both serious, and bothered. What had happened that spring in 1977 was shocking.

Ona Mae continued. "I had been at the Supper Club for a few years. Doing the same thing I do now. Outside of the big entertainment towns like New York, Los Angeles, and Chicago, that little place was something special. Even Dean Martin worked there," she said with a smile.

We hadn't said a word, so she continued, "The Beverley Hills Supper Club in Southgate, Kentucky, drew some of the finest entertainers and celebrities around. It was a well know place from coast to coast. Booking was never a problem, but

53

accommodating was. We often didn't have the room for the mass of people. Many times, dates filled up and we had to say no. We said no to great, young couples like you. That spring weekend was fully scheduled. We had every meeting room booked. Every hall was booked. The bigwig entertainer that night had the showroom packed over capacity. We could hardly get from point A to point B. Nobody could. It was going to be a great weekend for everyone there: staff, visitors, celebrities, you name it. It was a holiday weekend, a weekend that I will never forget."

I already couldn't take it and blurted out, "The Supper Club? Did somebody die?"

Ona Mae shook her head from side to side before finishing. "Nope. 'Someone' didn't die. Almost 200 people did though. And another couple hundred were hospitalized. It was a big fire. That was my craziest and saddest day in the business."

We all have those questions we ask that we wish we could take back. God knows I have said and wished for more things that I could have reckked or taken back more times than I can count. Jen though, was smarter than most her age. She typically would never open a wound like this. She was just keeping conversation and didn't know what else to do. You could see it in Ona Mae's eyes that remembering that day was painful. Typical, sweet Jen. She emphatically apologized over and over again. But I, just like an idiot, I kept on pressing.

"What the hell? Where is this place? In Kentucky you said? I've never heard of this. What started the fire? Anyone famous die?"

A bunch of insensitive questions, I know, but I didn't care. I thought that I was more than qualified to ask since I had witnessed my parents die in an accident several years ago. But hearing this helps bridge some gaps for me. It is something I need resolution on. As she continued her story, I had no idea that what I was about to hear would be so meaningful to me.

It was Jen who spoke next. "I'm so sorry. Let's please talk of something else. Jim gets a little worked up about these kinds of things."

We had walked in that hotel at 9:00 a.m. We were supposed to be there a little less than an hour. Ona Mae started her day showing a couple of soon to be newlyweds around the place. Jen and I had three other venues to visit that day, but we never made it to another location. Ona Mae was there just for the day to handle office business, but she'd agreed to show us around. Lucky us. We didn't leave until 4:00 later that afternoon.

Apparently, in the days and weeks following the tragic fire, along with the "accident" talk, were also those who claimed arson. The way the fire had started was a little fishy. All the employees of the property were interviewed. Some once, others several times. Ona Mae said she didn't know anyone personally who had died in the fire. She said it was the chaos and hysteria during the fire that was most troubling. People where running around everywhere. There wasn't a plan, and if there was, she said, it wasn't working. Exactly one hundred sixty-five people died directly because of that fire.

Both men and women who planned an evening out that night found themselves called upon for acts of heroism. She spoke of a fireman who was off duty that evening and out with his wife who had reacted in the fashion like he was employed to do. He pulled countless people from a double door that was packed with frantic bodies trying to escape and carried them off under each arm.

She spoke of a bus boy who escorted anyone he could find out of the building. The lights had gone off and the guests were lost. He walked those floors countless times and therefore knew every corner like the back of his hand. As soon as he got a group out, back in he went. Ona Mae said that he never stopped. She said he probably single handedly saved more people than anyone that night.

As she recounted the evening, she spoke about another

person who stood out in her mind. Apparently, she had never seen this man before. She wasn't quite sure what he was doing there. He wasn't an employee. She was sure of that. He didn't appear to be a guest. Most of the guests wore cocktail attire. Perhaps soemone with the entertainment? Probably not, he was just a standout.

"He wasn't dressed properly," she said. "This guy didn't belong, and the oddest part was his voice."

"His voice?" I asked.

"Yes, he had the oddest accent. It was English, but it wasn't from Kentucky. We were out in the lawn with a group of people and all kinds of conversations were going on. Like I said, it was hectic, and people were running around everywhere. He'd said something about the number of firemen that were working the scene. The minute he spoke, I knew he wasn't from around these parts."

Over the past few years I have talked with Jennifer no less than a few dozen times about what that park ranger said to me and my brothers. My grandfather repeated his story to Jen one day not long ago about him being a part of his group with the Navy. Even though Jennifer has always believed what I've said, I can always tell when someone has doubt. As Ona Mae continued her story about that terrible day, Jen and I sat there in disbelief. It's hard to imagine 165 people dying where an hour beforehand they were partying and having a wonderful evening with family and friends. That's exactly how "he" works though, death and destruction all around when you least expect it.

Ona Mae paused for a brief second during her story looked at us both, and then Jen asked Ona Mae, "Where do you think that man with the odd accent was from?"

She continued, "I thought I had heard his type of accent before. I guessed. I asked him if he was from someplace in Europe? He shook his head no. Maybe Australia? And again, he shook his head no. As I stood there for a brief second, I looked him right in the eyes not knowing what to guess next."

He stared back and responded to me with, "Nah, somewhere in the middle." And that was it. Now thinking about it, I can't really remember talking about much more. And funny thing, before I knew it, he was just up and gone.

Right then, the hairs on my arms raised and my hands went cold. Of course he was. That's exactly how cowards work. The devil is no different. "He" had done his deal, and now it was time to move on. I sat there for a minute equally shocked but also feeling confident. Confident that I hadn't lost my mind. This is the third time I've heard those exact words, "Somewhere in the middle."

After spending all day with Ona Mae, we wrapped up the deal and signed a check. I think we were all tired. Talking about death is painful and exhausting. Jen and I were getting married in late July and still had tons of work to do.

Ona Mae walked us out to our car and congratulated us on the coming wedding.

"I'll see you two in a couple months. God bless," she said with a smile and she walked off.

Jen and I hadn't said a word about her comment. As we drove off, we chatted a little about the place and about Ona Mae. I didn't bring up the comments about the stranger or his voice, but right in the middle of our conversation Jen blurted out, "What in the hell did she say? Right in the middle? Are you kidding me?"

I didn't know exactly how to respond. I bit down on my lip and nodded my head up and down and just kept driving. I wanted to say something, but what? I was troubled enough about that asshole, and now here he is again in my life. But I feel good that I haven't lost my mind. I felt validated now that Jen heard the story as well.

I sat back and drove. I could see the wheels turning in Jen's head. I knew she was feeling exactly the same way I felt years ago when I heard my grandfather repeat those exact words. Now it was her turn. She was feeling the same shock. I didn't ask, but she was questioning things about what had just gone down and the odds of it all.

Another few minutes of complete silence passed, she hit me with it, "Jim, you gotta do something."

That's all she said. I knew it, and now so did she. Hearing those words, a third time was not an accident. We both knew that I had to do something before "he" found me and my new family.

"Yeah, sweet pea, you're right, I gotta do something. I don't know what, but I'll do something."

1 Corinthians
Chapter 16 Verse 14

Let all that you do be done in love.

NIV

Chapter 7

Mad Max

March 14, 1993

LAST YEAR DURING SPRING AND SUMMER, Jen spent most of her time planning our wedding. Me? I spent the better part of that summer planning when and how I was going to track "him" down. Not one time in the past few years have I even come close. No signs, no pictures, no voices, and no trace of "him" anywhere.

Often, she became annoyed with me for helping less with the wedding and spending more time on other things. So, when Jen said my little quest was nothing more than an addiction I needed to rid, I of course said what I thought was obvious.

"I'm just having fun…my friends all enjoy hearing my stories of the places I've gone." Or, "I'm a hard-working guy, a good man, this isn't more important than you or anything else we are working on."

I wouldn't admit it to anyone, but several times I've thought and wished I had never started this, and I knew she was right. All the time spent looking for "him" and I can't prove to anyone what I believe is true. I'd be lying if I didn't admit I should probably find a way to stop this nonsense.

I've had a few buddies who have had addictions. One spent two months in the hospital for his drinking problem and the other spent a year in jail after his second DUI. I also knew a gambler. He was a great guy, a hard worker, and a wonderful family man who damn near lost it all just "having fun with his friends trying to get ahead." Then there are the slaves of tobacco. I know several people who have all shared that addiction, but I've never understood it. They spend all their money on the largest killer worldwide. All the folks I know who are addicted to tobacco, at some point all have said to me the same two things: "Jim, I wish I had never started," and "I can't seem to find a way to stop!"

Everywhere I go, I'm looking for "him." Everyone I talk to, I'm listening. Looking and listening for something. Anything. Every movie, television show, or book I read, I pay attention. He's out there somewhere. I know it, but where?

Recently while searching through some newspapers and hoping to find something, I read a story about a guy from Florida. The story was about felonies and those who commit them. This particular story was from some years back. This guy had a different kind of addiction. His addiction was bank robbery. He had hit over 40 banks in just a couple of years. It was his story that gave me an idea I hadn't thought of prior to my trips of looking for the devil.

Often when someone is on the run, say a bank robber, their names are unknown and someone else comes up with a nick name. Perhaps someone in law enforcement? Maybe one of the victims tells something about the crime just committed against them and they use a name that becomes a nick name. In this case, the media had given the bank robber the nick name, Mad Max.

He wore a white t-shirt, and everything else, from head to toe was black leather. Black hat, black jacket, pants, and boots.

Even his belt was black leather. He confidently went from bank to bank in his black mustang and carried a beat-up sawed-off shotgun that stuck out of his right jacket pocket. He looked like he belonged in a Hollywood action movie. He was the tough type with a five o'clock shadow and a prominent jaw line. His hair was also close to black, and his skin color was more on the tan side, than white.

Mad Max was robbing banks all over Florida. He was asking the tellers for everything in the drawer. He never hit more than one teller in the same bank. He also never went for the vault. Why? Probably because it kept things quick and easy.

Each teller that he robbed would all say the same thing. He used pleasant words like please and thank you. Often while robbing the teller, he'd smile at them. Almost flirting with the lady he was pointing a gun at. He always robbed female tellers. It was reported several times that the tellers claimed he winked at them during the hold up.

"If it wasn't for the fact that he was pointing a gun at me, I might have actually liked the guy," said one of the tellers from the article.

The reports read that Mad Max was "in and out in less than 30 seconds." In another story, he had finished the job in 15-20 seconds. This guy knew what he was doing. For over a year the police and FBI were scrambling, trying to catch up to Mad Max. He would hit a bank and the police would set-up roadblocks like a DUI check point. However, they were not looking for drunks, but rather a black mustang. He also always wore black leather gloves and never left clues behind to find. He would hit banks morning, noon, and afternoon on different days. Never any kind of a pattern for the authorities to follow. The police and other law enforcement had a lack of words and scratched their heads when asked about him. Trying to find him? They had nothing.

Something was odd about this man. An off-duty officer

happened to be in a bank once when Mad Max paid a visit. He said in his statement following the robbery that he had noticed the shotgun looked like it was missing a trigger. After that robbery, the authorities examined various tapes of prior hold-ups and noticed the same thing. That old shot gun didn't have a trigger. And not only that, but what looked like a metal strap was actually peeled up in one spot suggesting black electrical tape was used to hold the barrel together. Unreal, everyone thought. Mad Max was robbing banks with a toy gun, or better yet, some garage project gone bad.

Around the end of Mad Max's career, he hit a small bank in Melbourne, Florida. A little beach town on the eastern side of the state, south of Orlando. Again, he was in and out in 20-30 seconds. The teller he robbed was a native to the area for over 50 years. She did exactly what was asked of her.

Mad Max asked, "Please open the drawer and put all the cash you have in the bag."

The teller nervously handed over $3,200 dollars to Mad Max. As Mad Max said thank you to her, he gave his signature smile with a quick wink of the left eye. He swept out the door, and smoothly hopped into the running mustang on the curb. In and out before most of the customers and even the staff knew they had just been robbed.

The older teller, due to the commotion that Mad Max had caused, was taken to the emergency clinic across the street. She wasn't feeling well, probably nothing more than anxiety. She said his blue-eyed wink and smooth voice had given her a panic attack while he robbed her. After being released from the clinic an hour later, she went back to the bank to finish up interviews with the police.

The place was surrounded. Not just with cops, but with half of Melbourne outside the bank. The famous Mad Max was all over the TV and radio. I guess I can understand people's excitement for this kind of fanfare. Heck, I've driven all over the country looking for "satan." If anyone could understand the interest, it was me.

The teller had to weave her way through the large crowd after leaving the clinic. While crossing the street she bumped into a man. He was just one of the many locals trying to catch a look at the robbery scene. Nothing about him was unusual. Well, except one little thing.

After she bumped into him, she said, "Excuse me," and he said the same in politeness back to her. Very briefly they exchanged a smile and while passing and he winked at her from his left eye. This was the second time that she had been winked at in the past few hours. Funny, she told the police later that she hadn't been winked at twice in the last twenty years, much less the same day.

The teller was in the bank for just a few minutes with the authorities, but after her little story, the police got very interested in things outside the bank. From inside the bank through the glass walls, she pointed to a man outside whom like everyone else, was just watching the commotion. The same guy she had just bumped into. As the police and teller sat there and looked at him, they began to break down things about the guy. Height, weight, body style and so forth.

Believe it or not, there he was. Mad Max in person. Wearing a ball cap and the same white t-shirt from the robbery he had just committed. He was without the leather jacket, hat and had slipped on some blue jeans. He was just quietly there with hundreds of others. Just standing and waiting to see what was happening. What had been a search for almost two years would end that afternoon when Todd Vanhorn, also known as Mad Max, was surrounded by the police. He went quietly and with the same smile that had become his trademark.

This was my idea on how to find "satan." He was out there. Maybe he, like Mad Max, just liked to see what was going on. Mad Max confirmed it for me during his booking with the police department. Of course, he had plenty to say and acknowledge about all the banks he had hit. The interview went on for days. When the news finally reported the story, he was asked more than once why he was back at that bank that same day.

Todd said, "It's a damned addiction. I get a thrill out of seeing what I created."

Mad Max had returned to the scene of every single bank he had robbed. The guy ended up being as nice and polite as he was when robbing the banks. Always a please and thank you. Yes sir and no sir, was how he always spoke with the police. It was hard not to like the guy and when they asked where the money was, it was even harder. He had been robbing banks for almost two years to get money to help his dad's fight against cancer. He only took what was needed, and he needed it to help a loved one.

So, I thought, maybe that other idiot, satan, is doing the same thing. He might be returning to the scene of the crime to indulge in his doings. Maybe that's how I was going to catch him. Maybe in the crowd, maybe in a clinic across the street. I wasn't sure where, but I knew I could find him. I knew that people gathered. Graduations, funerals, birthdays, weddings, it doesn't matter. The number of people who visit the memorial at Pearl Harbor every year is over ten thousand. People return to a place of a horrific tragedy in history. But why?

For everyone it's different. Just like a criminal returning to the scene of the crime, perhaps satan "himself" took an opportunity to see the pain on the faces of God's children. The more I thought about it, I was sure of it. He didn't have the upper hand on anything. God is powerful. Satan is a wuss. What isn't possible with man, is possible with God. Satan's joy came from pain and destruction. The pain of people struggling, or better yet, the pain of God's children struggling.

I will continue looking for him following horrible acts of violence and disasters. There is and never has been a shortage of evil in the world. For a guy who as a kid couldn't stand reading in school, it became part of my daily routine. Reading newspapers, magazines, and watching too much TV became an everyday ordeal since that day my grandfather sat on the couch with my two brothers looking at that photo album.

He had reappeared to me that day with my brothers and Gramps. Maybe I could locate "him" in other pictures or film clips. I might be able to find him at the scene of something that happened. Newspaper reporters are everywhere. They print everything and I had to keep up with it all.

Day after day, week after week, and what was becoming year after year, the search for "him" has never stopped. Of course, I ended up putting myself through some lost leads and false hopes thinking, *Oh yeah...that's him!* even when it wasn't. I'd spend a week or two trying to find out the background behind some poor guy who I thought was satan.

Allen Greene was a business owner and family man who had once witnessed a car crash. The story was all over the news. Witnessed it my ass, I thought. He was there because he caused it. It was a bad accident in Arizona. A freak accident that should have never happened. An entire family and a church group in that van all died. Nine people total and Allen just happened to witness it? In the middle of an Arizona highway? Well, I didn't run to Arizona, but instead I started using my resources to track down old Mr. Greene. As it turns out, I spent plenty of time, almost 30 hours a week on that story for over a month. Every free minute I had I spent looking at Allen from afar. And in the end? Mr. Greene wasn't "him."

Allen was on business in Arizona and had a family back home. The story read that he was a God loving man. I spent more than a month trying to make sure he was satan before I told the rest of the free world.

Unfortunately, this wasn't the only excursion I put myself through. I was always just sure that what I was looking at was "him." Each time, just as soon as I had the proof, one little detail always presented itself. Each time it was never the outcome I was looking for. Can you image how seriously people would take me if I accused that poor man? This was an addiction for sure. Jen, my family, my friends, and anyone else I knew all agreed.

It was about this time in my life that I thought about how nice it would be to find "him" and get over this. My son was getting to an age where sports and quality time with Dad were becoming more and more important. For the both of us. Trying to juggle a job, a family, and this addiction was not possible. I could never get as much time as I wanted to spend with my family. I always longed for more.

One Sunday at church, the pastor was teaching from the book of Proverbs and spoke about God's plan for each person and the events that take place in your life to create direction. He spoke about a path in life and how we tend to question the path we are on. Good, bad, or different, it's God's plan, not ours. Just keep moving forward with the faith that God does have a plan for you.

Something about those words resonated with me. God *does* have a plan for me, I thought. I have always felt a calling to my madness. For some odd reason, I can't really say why, I have to continue and catch "him." I wondered if there was a way I could figure out a plan of where "he" would be next and get there before he does. I wonder throughout history how many men have also been tasked with this same question.

Ephesians
Chapter 5 Verse 6

Let no one deceive you with empty words,
for because of such things God's wrath comes
on those who are disobedient.

NIV

Chapter 8

Living Another Lie

April 1993

IT HAS BEEN ALMOST 20 YEARS, and I still pray every night. There are not many nights that I don't think about something that makes me restless. It's usually a news story, a blinding light, or the little stresses in life that keep me awake. Most nights it's that memory of my parents' death. Some nights it's for a few minutes, others it is for hours on end. Occasionally, it's all night. Almost twenty years later and I'm still waiting for a good night's sleep.

After the accident in the hills, my grandmother spent the bulk of her time with me and my brothers. Since becoming a parent again, you'd never know her age. Her being fifty something, at the time of the accident, the three of us sure kept my grandparents active. The bulk of that time was right after dinner until each of us fell asleep. My grandmother spent her evenings with us. For my youngest brother, a little singing and maybe some TLC was all it ever took for him to be asleep in minutes. Maybe his young age meant he didn't understand the circumstances, or maybe it was just easier for him to forget. My middle brother was always high strung and hyper. A bath and a good book were his ticket to sleep. I was a different story though.

My mental image of the camper bursting into flames during my parents' death just won't leave my mind. I can still see exactly what my mom and dad were doing. I still see their faces and the look on my mother's face as she was about to say something to me. I sometimes think she is still saying something to me now, but I just can't make out what it is. My mother's face had a look on it like she knows you can't hear her, but she has something to say anyway. Maybe she was warning me of something seconds away from happening to her and my dad. She was warning me that "he" was down the road and coming our way. During a typical day my friends and family would keep me active. Losing that image was easier with the distractions, but at night, there it was, just like it had happened yesterday.

"We pray on our time. Answers from God are on his time." I'll never forget one of Grandma's best quotes. I think I heard them all a hundred times, but that one I heard, understood, and remembered from day one. She helped me understand the power of prayer. Grandma must have asked me once a week while I was living with them to recite Matthew 21:22. "If you believe, you will receive whatever you ask in prayer." She never stopped asking until she felt positive that I not only knew it, but I also used it in my life. We started praying the night of the accident. I was only a teenager, and my attitude was of course: I knew everything. At the time I was a decent athlete and a good student. I thought of myself as one of those tough kids. I could handle anything. After losing my parents, I quickly found out how tough I wasn't.

My parents always had one of my brothers or me say grace. That didn't change when we moved in with Grandma and Grandpa. We never ate a single meal without saying thank you. Growing up, we went to church here and there. That's probably one of my earliest memories. Not church really but putting on those damn sweaters that itch you to death. I knew back then that if I ever had a son, his mother would not make him wear one of those sweaters. Back then I'd tell you it was church I hated on Sundays, but now I'll tell you it was that damn sweater.

But church, grace, and prayer in general has and still is a part of "my thing." It was just what Christian folks do I guess, and it is a part of who I am. I don't have a single memory of any instructions or a "How To" lesson, but praying was a part of life for me as a kid. Most times, like any other kid, when I was in trouble it was, "Oh God, please let me get that grade," or "Oh Lord, please don't let my dad find out." Today, it is, "God, please let this or let that happen." I'm not sure of most things, but I'm very sure that praying will be part of my life until the day I die.

My grandmother was great. We prayed for understanding and strength when we were weak. We asked for help and guidance when we were lost. We asked for help for those in our lives with their struggles. Grandma believed praying for loved ones or for friends is something Jesus would want us to do. We also prayed for those we didn't know. The old, the poor, and the sick. It didn't matter where they were, who they were, or why they were like that. Praying to help those less fortunate than us was the first step to helping anyone. Of course, most nights back then and often still today, I always ask for a little help getting to sleep.

There are churches all over the world with different religions, different beliefs, and different lifestyles, but they all pray or have some variation of time spent with themselves and the person in charge. For me, Jesus Christ is the man. Everyone I run into, if it's appropriate, I'll tell them all I know about the nutty carpenter who can walk on water.

It was in church one Sunday a few weeks back that we first prayed for this other nut. Or better yet, we prayed for those surrounded by this nut. This fella in Waco, Texas had convinced several followers of his church, The Branch Davidian, to hold up in their compound outside of the city. Sad to say, but several members of his cult as well as some authorities ended what should have been a simple legal paper exchange, with a gun battle. The news reported ten people killed. A few weeks ago, I was just hearing of this guy and his cult, and now I'm learning all I can about The Branch Davidian.

For an unnecessary reason, many people are dead. This story became the headline in every newspaper and TV news program out there. For me, this is perfect. Exactly the attention and commotion that normally has "him" somewhere around. If my theory is right, he'll be hanging out in the crowd. The crowds of interested and concerned citizens are congregating in the area, and I'm almost positive that he will be there. Just like Mad Max, I really believe that he will be in the crowd looking at his handy work and making his future plans. At minimum, he will be spending time with the crowd making small talk. Probably recruiting under the radar. Posing as some concerned citizen blabbing about why God would let this happen. I can hear him now, "If there really is a God, how could he let these innocent people die?" Blah, Blah, Blah. "God isn't here, God doesn't save you, God is the problem."

I have been watching TV, scanning the radio and reading the newspapers high and low for a glimpse of "him," but have found nothing. Most of the coverage is about the FBI's growing mobilization. What had been a couple officers trying to serve a warrant the other day is turning into hundreds of officers, guns, and helicopters surrounding the area. A regular war zone. To tell you the truth, I really don't know what The Branch Davidian is all about. A bunch of nuts thinking aliens or another higher power is going to take them away? Away where? Who knows? I really don't care. As sad as these deaths have been, if experiencing this is what it takes to find "him," then so be it.

Now, the tough part. I've got to get to Waco.

Jen is never going to let me go. As much as it pains me, I've come up with a story she might believe. Coincidentally, I told her about six months ago that the owners of my restaurant are looking at other locations. That's true they are looking at other locations throughout the south, even in Texas. This would be my way in.

I'm going to tell Jen that plans with the restaurant to expand are taking on steam. I can't just tell her I'm heading to Waco. She'll never buy it. But rather, I would have to drive through most of Texas to hit Waco. There are several towns along the way. Little Rock, Dallas, and Fort Worth which are all legitimate places the restaurant could expand. If I were really driving to and from Kentucky to all those places, including Waco and then Houston it would sound more like a completed round trip. This will buy me some time to do some site seeing at the compound. Site seeing for "him" that is. I hate to lie to her, but Jen understands that I truly believe "he" is out there. Unfortunately, Jen still doesn't understand why I need to find "him."

Once I do find "him" everything will be alright. I can tell her what I did and why I did it. But for now, this little white lie won't harm her. Who knows, once I do find "him," what good this will do for our family. How cool would it be to tell the story about tracking him down? I could even sell this story on TV or for a movie. Maybe the title will be "Running with the Devil" or something fun. It will be my story about finding the biggest perpetrator of crime, hate, rage, destruction, and death in the history of the human race. Yeah, that would solve things at home.

It was Monday night and my story to Jen was set. Right before dinner I would mention how my boss wants to "maybe send me" on a little trip. We'd eat, play a board game with the kids, and hit bedtime early. That was the first part of the plan. Early the next morning I would call her from work and tell her that my boss confirmed the trip, and I'd be leaving bright and early Friday morning for my 770-mile drive.

As I was teeing up the execution of my plan, Jen reminded me during dinner that she had already made plans for Friday and Saturday. I had completely forgotten that she'd been planning on helping a girlfriend set-up a garage sale that they would both be working on all weekend. She rolled her eyes at me as if it was so typical that I would forget.

After dinner that evening Jen asked, "Jim what is wrong with you?" As I was running through every scenario possible of how I could get to Waco.

"Nothing Jen. Just a lot of stuff at work. My boss actually asked if I could do that road trip into Texas and look at those sites he told me about. Remember I told you about his expansion plans?"

"Oh, Jim, I feel bad. I'd really like to help, but you know I've been planning on this for over a month."

"No, no problem. It's not on you. I'm just annoyed at him for pushing the issue. I told him we have plans and this weekend was no good. He just needs to deal with it. After all, I told him any other weekend but this one would work."

As usual, Jen was great. She is always understanding and helpful to solve a problem. I feel guilty. The dozen of lies in the past four hours that I weaved myself into is shameful. It's sad that I have to live this way. At least my trip to Waco was in my control now, and maybe will be set for future weekends.

I continued to try and plan out the trip, but it was not working out. For one reason or another: work, the kid's activities, Jennifer's plans, whatever...I couldn't see on the schedule for at least a month until I could get to Waco. The media was still covering the standoff and the FBI was running the show at the cult's hideout, or at least that was what was being reported.

I watched TV and read every article printed about the issue. The more I read and caught on TV, the more I thought I've lost my chance. "He" has probably already come and gone. This crap in Waco was going on now for almost two months and at some point, these nuts inside the compound are going to walk right out. The leader of this group, well, he might die in a standoff with police, but was I really going to drive almost 800 miles to see more idiots die? I don't think so.

I had a normal shift on Wednesday at the restaurant where nothing out of the ordinary happened. Wednesday was also one of the few nights that I could unwind by going to the gym. However, Jen was at home when my boss called. She didn't answer the phone but listened to the message left by my boss instead.

"Jim, sorry to bother you at home, but I need to discuss something with you as soon as you can. Call me at the restaurant please. Tell your pretty wife I say hello."

At about 6:40 in the evening I walked in the house and Jen told me to listen to the answering machine. I stepped outside on the back deck when I made the call.

"Jim, we've been stung."

"Stung how?"

"There was one of those BS sting operations run by the local cops with the liquor board. About 45 minutes after you left, one of our servers, Danielle served a cocktail to a 20-year-old minor and she never asked for an ID."

"You have to be kidding me. What the hell is going to happen now? Danielle is one of our best servers. Do we pay a fine or what?"

"It's way worse than that Jim. Not only is there a fine, but they are filing the paperwork with the liquor board tomorrow, and starting next Sunday the restaurant has to serve a 72-hour no liquor sale for a penalty. One of the owners might even have to go to court."

We talked for 15 minutes to discuss our game plan. Jen had come outside a few times trying to listen in. She could tell through the window that something had happened. As we chatted, we talked about reducing hours or cutting back staff for the weekend. Seventy-five percent of our weekly sales were from the weekend and of those sales, 35% is in alcohol. Even if we only sold food, with labor and other fixed costs, we might *actually lose* money opening the doors. After wrestling with the issue, we decided it might be best to close Saturday night and re-open Wednesday morning as usual. Later that night, I realized I had my way for a quick trip to Waco.

Jen and I were watching TV when the usual coverage of the standoff was on the local news. One of the local reporters brought up the daily events, just as they did in most of the prior days and weeks. Nothing really of interest though. Occasionally, the cult's leader made promises to come out or to let some of his followers leave. Neither resulted in anything. While I was at the gym earlier that night, and while my staff was serving cocktails to minors, there was one statement from the compound that caught my ear.

Earlier that day while one of the negotiators spoke with the leader at the compound, he was quoted as calling it the "Ranch Apocalypse." Jen and I both heard the same thing, but she was the first to say it.

"Apocalypse? Do you think he really said that?"

"Ah yeah, guessing from what they have said about this nut and his Branch Davidian, I'm sure he has them all wired crazy."

"Crazy is one thing, but an apocalypse, Jim? That's the end. Their leader is telling us that the end is coming!"

Every hair on my body stood up. I didn't say another word on the subject. I sat in bed with Jen watching the rest of the news. My mind was going wild with ideas. What are the odds that we just heard about the apocalypse? What are the odds that it came from this whack job? That's exactly how "he" works, walking around like a lion to find the weak in order to devour them. This asshole in Waco was claiming that aliens might be heading this way and now the end is near? Also, what are the odds that just a few hours ago, the restaurant was being shut down for the weekend?

Neither of us were asleep yet and Jen asked, "So, now what are you planning on doing with your free weekend?"

"Well, I have all kinds of things on my mind" I replied.

"Oh really, like what?" She asked.

"Well. There is a lot to do in the office at the restaurant." That was a lie.

"I was also just thinking of getting some work done around here in the garage and the yard." Oh, that was definitely a lie. It sounded good, but that thought never actually crossed my mind.

I also included one last lie, "When I was speaking with my boss tonight, he did mention that this might be the perfect time to head to Texas and check out those sites. After all, I wouldn't have to miss any work this weekend if I went."

I had no idea where this one was going or how Jen would take it.

"Well, Jim, that actually makes sense. He's been bothering you like mad to get you to go."

"Yeah, but..."

"No, seriously. You couldn't go last month, and this is something he probably needs," she continued.

"Well, what about..."

"Jim, I also think this may help your career."

"Yeah, I thought about that, but..."

"Jim, you're going! I've made up your mind."

"Yeah, honey, maybe you're right, I probably should go."

Just like that, the trip to Waco was back on. It was perfect to, it was Jen's idea now, not mine. I still feel guilty about how it went down, but this will all pay off one day. And on that day we will sit around and laugh about how I set the bait. She went for it all: the hook, line, and sinker! If I was fishing today, I would have just caught a record breaker!

The next morning, I had to work as usual. The morning staff wasn't aware of last night's deal and they also didn't know they were getting a three-day weekend. Typically in restaurants, that's not much of a problem. I spoke to the boss late on Thursday morning and told him his store was all set for the three-day forced vacation. Unfortunately, I had to BS him as well. I didn't want to risk getting a call to the house again this weekend. I told him I had family in Texas and wanted to take a quick trip there to say hello. I called the assistant manager in early so I could be on the road after lunch.

I had to hit home quickly to grab a change of clothes and my road meals. The kids were in school and Jen was home alone. Unlike so many previous trips, this one was coming together nicely. No work, Jen was on board, and the weather was good. Maybe with any luck, "he" will be there. Something is in store for me, I can feel it. Everything was going as expected.

That is, until I walked through the front door at home. What I wasn't expecting was Jen at the top of the staircase just getting out of the shower. I could see her dark curly hair, eight inches past her neckline. Her big brown eyes and her skin color with its golden tint that drove me wild. She was wearing a white t-shirt that was just barely big enough to cover everything.

"Ready to go?" is all she asked.

"Yeah..." I said with a boyish grin.

"What are you doing for dinner with the kids tonight?" I continued slowly.

"Well actually, nothing. I'm home alone until later. One of the neighborhood moms invited the kids to a get together with all the neighbors. I guess they're going to get pizza. Chrissy, from across the street, is going to get them from school and take them. I won't need to pick them up until after 8:00."

She paused. "So, like I said, I'm home alone until then." This time she was grinning.

I didn't say another word. Neither did she. She stood there staring, flirting with me.

"I need to go turn the truck off," I said.

As I returned outside, Waco never even entered my mind. I couldn't have cared less. I was out the door and back inside again in mere seconds. Jen wasn't standing on top of the staircase when I came back inside, but I had a good idea where she was.

As I made my way up the stairs, I noticed the same white t-shirt was on the floor. It never made it into our bedroom.

It wasn't just two minutes of play like the usual act we put on. It was hours of love making. Too often it is just a few minutes here, maybe a weekend morning there. Something was always going on, or someone was always tired. The whole process of years into a marriage is too often a routine that eventually gets skipped. Not today. We tore into each other like crazed teenagers. A little after 7:00 we decided to go out and grab a quick bite to eat. Both of us went to get the kids from the neighbor's house on the way home. Heck, I was already home. There was no need to rush out of town now. Putting the kids to bed seemed completely natural.

As it turned out, Jen put me to bed as well. Why not just get up and head out early in the morning, well rested and knowing that my family would be fine when I left them. Jen and I watched the news in bed and snuggled. Jen's favorite.

The alarm went off and I was dressed and out the door in a minute. The clock in my truck read 3:59 a.m. when I backed out the driveway.

I made it to Waco in about 12 hours. Boy, Texas is a big place. My path wasn't the town to town path I had told Jen I was going on. It was more of a straight shot to Waco. Seeing how this trip actually came together so quickly, I didn't do the research into exactly where the compound was. As I approached the city limits, I thought it might be just as easy to ask some kid at a convenience store where the "nuts" were located. Maybe I could tell them I was working with the press and had to meet over there. Who would really care anyways? I could find it.

What I did find was a Piggly Wiggly or Wiggly Piggy or something. I don't know. Just a gas station with a convenience store inside. The person working the counter was an older gal, maybe 60 something. A southerner with big hair and a strong accent.

"Hey Ma'am, would you happen to know how to get to that compound where the FBI and all the news crews are at?

"The Branch Davidian group sweetie. Those folks?" She replied.

"Yeah, I work for a news group from Kentucky and need to get something to one of our camera men."

"Just horrible what happened, ain't it?

"Yeah, it is. Hopefully they'll get it under control and end this crap," I remarked.

"Well, after what happened today, I'm not sure The Branch Davidian will have any other followers," she said shaking her head.

Angie was the name on her ID tag. She knew exactly how to get to the compound. I wrote out the directions, but I could almost recall what she had said from memory. I returned to the cab of my truck and stopped briefly. I froze as I recalled something Angie had said just a minute earlier. "Well after what happen today, I'm not sure The Branch Davidian will have any other followers." What the hell does that mean? I wondered.

I got back out of the truck and went back inside.

"Ma'am, what did you mean, after what happened today?"

"Well, the fire. Haven't you heard? It's on all the stations."

"No. I've driven 12 hours just listening to CD's in my truck. What happened today?" I said impatiently.

"Well, hun, the FBI tried to force their way into the building and them Branch Davidian folks burned the place to the ground."

"My God, you have got to be kidding me? So they just all came out and then the building burned to the ground?" I asked, perplexed.

"Nope. Someone started that fire and every soul inside, every man, woman, and child died today. It just makes me angry. I feel so sad for those poor children." Shaking her head side to side, her eyes were a little misty, she was done talking. I left the store for the second time, but this time floored with anger.

I had my hand-written directions and was off to the compound. I wasn't driving as quickly or as eagerly as I had been the last 700 miles. This morning at 4:00 I was so excited about the trip and about possibly finding "him," but right now? I felt sick. The last 20 miles seemed to take forever. As I approached the area there were roadblocks in every direction. Sometimes the roads would have a high spot where I could get a glance, but I saw nothing but headlights and fire trucks around what looked like the site. It was dark and I don't think anybody would see me if I stayed the night. This would be a good time to find a place to sleep and have at it again in the morning.

I met the morning sun wide awake. I hadn't slept well in my truck. For the second time in 24 hours I watched the radio flash 3:59 a.m. However, this morning was nothing at all like the morning I had yesterday. Thinking about it, what if I wouldn't have spent the night with Jen? I would have been here for the fire. Security was tight, but now it's almost impossible to get close. Even to photograph anything would be a stretch. From the right hilltop the distance might be a mile or so, if not further. Did I blow my chance? Now that I think about it, was this the plan? Maybe the restaurant being shut down wasn't an accident? I was supposed to be here to witness this! I was supposed to be here. Damn it!

I sat in the truck driving around, trying to gain any access I could. Nothing. I spent the entire Saturday morning and most of the afternoon getting nowhere driving around in circles. I'm not sure if missing the event was more disheartening, or the fact that this religious cult actually set their house on fire while they were still inside.

There were papers from the city of Waco and Dallas. I grabbed both. I sat in a hotel parking lot in my front seat and read what I could stomach. I read more about The Branch Davidian and their leader than I could stand. The more I read, the more I wanted to find "him." Yet another example of the devil getting ahold of the wrong person. That wrong person took "his" lead and walked almost 100 souls to their death.

Sitting here, I'm not sure what to do. I know I've wasted my time coming. I was eight hours too late. Nothing matters really, because innocent people are dead. There is nothing that I, nor anyone else could do about it. The sun was heading west. After a quick prayer for a safe trip back home, it was about time I headed back east.

Matthew
Chapter 26 Verse 52

Jesus said to him, "Put your sword back into its place. For those who take the sword will perish by the sword."

NIV

Chapter 9

Oklahoma City

April 1995

BACK IN HIGH SCHOOL I REMEMBER WATCHING "The Grapes of Wrath." Just a movie one of my teachers had us watch in a history class. I struggled to follow the plot, and the movie was in black and white. Oh, the pain! All I remember today about the movie, is people traveling across the country struggling the entire way in wagons pulled by horses. Some of the people traveled on horseback and some just walked across the land by foot. I also remember all of them were traveling in a never-ending dust storm.

When I arrived in Oklahoma City, I felt the same experience. I didn't ride into town on a horse like the movie, but I had the same perspective. Dust was everywhere. I'm not sure if the it was normal or if it was caused from the explosion. Maybe a combination of both perhaps? Dust was on every window of every building and car within miles of the site.

I left Jen and the kids the night of the bombing at 6:00 p.m. She was less than happy about it, but oh well. I hate to have that attitude, but she knew about this prior to us officially dating.

After we "discussed it," I was mentally ready to roll, and was packed to leave right after dinner.

The drive to the blast area took about 11 hours. I drove all night and took a little nap for about an hour along the way. I arrived the following morning right at sunrise to a scene out of a movie, but no black and white version this time. This was in full color. The lights from the emergency vehicles and police cars could be seen for miles. As a matter of fact, emergency vehicles and black SUVs were the only cars you could find for blocks in every direction.

As I approached the site, people were scrambling everywhere. Heavy equipment vehicles and fire trucks surrounded the immediate area around the building. Outside of that were multiple rows of police cars and ambulances. In between the two, were emergency personnel. There must have been 200 nurses, doctors, fireman; heck, I even saw guys wearing OKC sanitation shirts in the mix trying to help. From an outsider's point of view, this was chaos. But from the perspective of a guy who's been following "him" from one hell hole to another, I could tell this was as organized as it could be during an emergency.

My view wasn't going to work for my need. I needed a point to observe the scene, maybe from a parking garage or one of the other buildings in the area. I spent the bulk of the morning trying to gain access to a better point of view. I was dressed pretty light. Just some pants and a light jacket. I was carrying only my binoculars and my camera.

I spent four hours, seriously the better part of the morning trying to find my viewing spot. The law enforcement personnel and emergency workers seemed to have the only access to anywhere I wanted to be. I continued to circle around, up and down the side streets. Every time I thought I'd found a way in, I ran into a police officer or a dead end. It was almost lunchtime by the time I found my opening.

Just to the north of the blast sat a three-story Oklahoma

water research building. It was decently sized with many offices. It might offer a great view as a roof-top access if I could just get in the building.

In my circle around the blast site, I was north of the water building and noticed people going in and out the door adjacent to a parking lot. I knew if "he" was here, this building might be my only chance to view "him" from above and maybe run "him" down. The scene around the building was locked down for several blocks in every direction. In less than 24 hours, they had turned this into the largest crime scene in history. As I approached the door to the building about ten feet away, it swung open. I had my way in.

Two people walked out with yellow wind breakers on. On the upper left chest was OKC in big letters with something written below. There was a man and a woman, neither of them seemed to notice or even care that I was dressed in a black jacket, blue jeans, and sun glasses. I'm not sure what they were doing, but I had a good feeling they belonged there. I was just there to check things out.

As I reached for the door, I fully expected to be met by a check point of some kind or at minimum an officer standing inside. I had my excuse, or "lie" ready when asked why I was there. I opened the door to find a fire escape. Not a single person was there. I headed in, far too easily, in my honest opinion.

I wanted to get up to the top floor first. The side of the building I was on was in good condition. It was on the north side, opposite of the same street as the blast area. Other than being a little dated, I might not have noticed what had happened on the opposite side. The offices facing north were fairly undamaged. I went into a couple bathrooms and found a cracked mirror. Other than that, nothing of interest. The south side however, was a completely different story.

The first office door that I tried to open was jammed shut. I put my shoulder into the door and could feel the it move, but it felt like I was moving piles of brick behind the door. It was about three doors down that I noticed another office with an opened door. I could see the daylight glaring into the hallway. No lights were on in the building. As I approached the door, I could hear the chaos outside. Alarms, sirens, dogs barking, voices screaming, and the sound of collapsing cement.

I turned to my right and immediately saw at an office turned upside down. The window was opposite of the door and I could see that the south side of the building was completely gone. Not a single shard of glass was in the window frame. Not a single piece. Furniture was destroyed, and wallpaper was peeled off the walls. One photo remained hanging, which was odd as everything else was destroyed. As I walked across what was once an office, and the scale of the destruction outside became more visible. I walked to the edge of the window and stood motionless as I stared and watched. I didn't move from my spot for an hour.

The damage was something like I'd never seen before. The pile of rubble was maybe seven or eight stories tall. How the rest of the building was still standing was unbelievable. I could have sat there all day watching the emergency efforts. Ladders and crew with hard hats were everywhere and on every level crawling around rebar, concrete, electrical cables, glass, and metal that had been sheared off. I never took a single picture of the building itself. I was there to find "him." As I stood there, I thought I wouldn't ever want to remember or look at this scene again.

After an hour or so of standing at the window I decided to get to work. There were some offices just east with a little better view of the site. I went into any room I could. Each was the same, destruction you couldn't even imagine. I was there for well over an hour and the afternoon seemed to bring on several more visitors. I knew the clock was ticking. I had to find a good observation point to get some photographs. The building was filling up with all kinds of officials doing their work. I was probably the only one who had no real reason for being there.

I tried to gain access to the roof, but those doors were locked. I made it downstairs to the second level and much was the same. The north offices were okay, but the south offices looked like hell. I started to get nervous about the number of police and FBI jackets I saw. *Act like you belong there, and move like you know where you are going, you might go unnoticed,* I kept repeating in my head. Well as it turns out, I was in that water building for over six hours before the sun finally set. Not a single person asked what I was doing there.

I did have a conversation with one guy though. I was on level three taking photographs of the crowd and behind me in walked a state trooper. Not only did he alarm me by being an officer, but he also asked me a question that I wasn't expecting.

"Anything worth photographing out there?" he asked.

Needing to keep the conversation normal, I replied, "Not really. Can you believe that mess?"

He approached me as I was still facing outside and came up to my immediate left.

"I served in Vietnam and thought I would never again see what I had experienced there. But this is bad. I can't believe it," he said.

Now the trick to going unnoticed in a crime scene is talking like you need to be there. Although I was nervous, I've been through this before. Keep calm and keep busy. All the while remembering not to ask anything that might lead to a question asked like, "What are you doing?" or "Who do you work for?" If I get those questions asked, I have to either make up a believable lie or get busted.

"Can you believe these offices?" I asked with a truly shocked look on my face.

"Yeah this morning at the station when we received our assignment for the day, I was a little miffed being assigned to the property next door. What the heck am I going to do over there, I thought. Now being here, holy cow!" the trooper replied while shaking his head.

I was trying to find a reason to leave when he asked me the next question.

"You been here all day?"

"Kind of. Arrived just a few hours ago, actually," I said.

"Seen anything over here worth mentioning?" he asked.

"Yeah, actually just ran across something you have to see to believe and after you see it, you still won't believe it!" After a slight delay I continued and asked, "You got a camera?"

Sure do, down in the squad car. Maybe only a few pictures left on the film, but we use it for crime scenes, and I could probably get away using the film for something worthwhile," he told me.

"Well how'd your boss take it if you were taking pictures on that camera for yourself? You know, for personal reasons. I mean if that film was to disappear and you actually developed those pictures to keep maybe for yourself. Possibly keep them for the rest of your life?" I asked.

"Well son, if you're suggesting I do something illegal, that isn't going to happen. Why would you ask that?" he said perplexed.

"Well friend, just be prepared that's all. What I'm about to show you is so unbelievable that you may not be able to let it go, EVER," I told him.

His face was a mixture of perplexation and intrigue. He paused for a brief second and said, "I'll be right back."

He turned and walked briskly away. I thought about escaping. This is the perfect time to disappear. I'd been pressing my luck being in the building this long already. However, this office was a fairly good vantage point for crowd watching. If "he" was down below, this might be my best spot to find him. I wasn't going to give it up unless I was forced to leave.

The office I was standing in was like most of the others on the south side. Office furniture of all shapes and sizes were pressed against doors and walls opposite of the windows. Some turned over, upside down, and most of it damaged. Fish tanks, computers, file cabinets, everything was destroyed. Diplomas, pictures from desks or walls, inspirational posters, all of them now on the floor. Almost nothing survived on that side of the building.

I wasn't sure if the trooper was coming back. I stood close to the window and continued photographing everyone. Rescue workers, fireman, and police officers are the toughest. They look a lot alike and are often hidden by hats and helmets. If "he" was there, it might be tough to notice. There were a lot of authority figures down below. Local and state police, FBI, ATF, and many others I couldn't recognize, but I knew the style: suits and sunglasses.

The more I thought about it, I don't think "he" would be posing as someone working down below. He would be in the crowds like Mad Max was. Hanging out and spectating. Checking out his handy work. I'm thinking he's probably wearing a white tee shirt, blue jeans, maybe a sports coat with that cocky grin on his face. I've been looking all day for a guy with his arms crossed, smiling from ear to ear at the hell sitting before him.

All afternoon, I scanned the crowds. I probably shot 300 pictures. A few times I got excited about a guy in the crowd. I studied him for a few minutes, but nothing. It wasn't him. Lots of on-lookers scattered around the site. Several folks came in to help. Oklahoma is the heart of the Bible belt and most folks in these parts are kind and helpful to a fault.

"I've got it," said the trooper as he reentered the room.

"Okay, take a look around the room. See anything odd?" I asked.

For two or three minutes the trooper looked around in a circle. He didn't say a word or ask a single question. He turned over some furniture, and moved some of the debris away from the walls. He was trying to find what it was that I mentioned might be so unbelievable. I could tell he was done with the guessing game and just at the moment, he noticed it. He looked up and right in front of him, there it was.

"That picture?" he asked.

I didn't answer him but rather said, "Follow me."

I led the trooper in and out of every office that had that picture in it. Maybe not the exact picture, but the same kind of picture. After about the fourth room, he had the same questions and felt the same oddity that I had when I discovered it. We spent an hour going into most offices in levels two and three. It was always the same thing. Walking together we found even more pictures than what I originally found earlier in the day.

"Who put these there? There is no way every other picture hit the floor and only these survived hanging on a wall or still upright on a desk. Someone had to have hung these last night or sometime this morning." It was so odd for the officer he was already making up excuses and trying to explain it in his head.

"I thought the same thing at first," I said. "However, after I thought about it, maybe someone either placed these there or went from office to office re-hanging them on the walls. Oh. And just one other thing I couldn't figure out."

"What's that?" the trooper inquired with an eager voice.

"The dust. Either from the blast or from poor cleaning over time. Every single one of these pictures hanging in all these offices has some dust on them. If you were hanging pictures, or picking them up off the floor, would you really hang up a dirty one? Even a fingerprint would have marked up a dusty frame. My point is, they are dusty from hanging here. Nobody has touched them."

"Yeah... yeah that's odd. Not nearly as odd as who's in the picture though. Kind of makes me feel funny just being here. You have a good evening young fella." And without another word, the officer turned around and left the building. He just left like he'd seen a ghost. I never even got his name.

In my truck later, I sat in the same parking lot thinking about my plan for tomorrow. It was too dark to be in that building anymore and I hadn't found him yet. I didn't have a room, but

I had some food and the weather wasn't bad. I could manage tonight in the truck. I sat and listened to the local radio. The airwaves were full of talk shows and other stations playing tributes and homage to yesterday's events. One of the local stations had a plea from the local police department for folks to keep away from the blast zone. Although many of those folks wanted to help, there were too many to manage. The chaos with trained professionals looked daunting enough.

I sat there flipping from station to station. There was a lot of talk about yesterday's event and a lot of rage and anger. Peppered in the calls were a few comments about political, racial, and religious opinions, but one call was about free will.

One guy called in and hammered the DJ that God was the responsible party for all of this. He rambled on for what seemed like an eternity about why and how God could let this happen. On and on. He had a few fair points and was obviously educated, but the rambling wouldn't end. Finally, the DJ having had enough himself, said thanks for calling, and cut him off.

Her name was Kelley. About 30 minutes following the "nut job," Kelley called in. She had a very soft and sweet voice. She sounded like a mature woman, maybe in her late 30s. She used please and thank you and at one point she even said pardon me, when she didn't hear something. You could tell from her voice alone that she was a southern lady.

She told the DJ that she had never called a TV or radio station before but after listening to the "nut" sometime before, she just had to call in. She had something to say.

Kelley asked the DJ if he understood or knew what "free will" meant. Or even if he could accurately describe it. The DJ wasn't going to fall for that trap.

"I have an idea or maybe even an opinion, but why don't you go ahead and tell us," the DJ respond.

Kelley started, "If you asked the average person what God's greatest gift is, what would they say?"

There was complete silence, the DJ wasn't about to interrupt.

"You might hear about love. That's the easiest answer. I believe just about every book in the Bible talks about love. Others might say, God's greatest gift was his son, Jesus Christ, and it's hard to argue with that one. Jesus came to teach us. In the end, he gave us all a lifetime of forgiveness through his death. I believe though, his greatest gift is that of free will.

"Long before the nightmare of yesterday here in Oklahoma City, long before any other human acts of violence or destruction, and before Jesus was crucified, humans still existed. So really, you have to start at the beginning. From the beginning, Adam and Eve were given everything they wanted. They had only one rule. They didn't have any commandments, no laws, nobody to hide to explain their actions to. They had one rule. Don't eat from this tree!

"Free will, God's greatest gift to his creation of man, allows each and every one of us to make the best of where we are and what we are doing. Free will is truly the only real separation amongst us all. Some think skin color, wealth, or religious beliefs separate the masses. But that is false.

"Free will is different. Pick your favorite time in history. I love the one I'm living in. The past 80 years in our American history is my favorite. How far we have come in such a short time. I love people like Gandhi, Mother Theresa, and President Kennedy. All with visions, all with dreams, and all with hope for a better world.

"Adolph Hitler, Charles Manson, and whoever did this horrible thing downtown were driven by free will. Why would you load a truck with explosives and kill so many people? Why? Probably for the same reason others might try loving so many people. It's free will. Some use it for the good of man, or to write a work of art, or paint a beautiful picture. Others use it to tear something down. To kill without conscience and to harm without reason."

Kelley spoke a while longer. Her point was made and she was never interrupted. I hoped all of Oklahoma City was listening. After she finally said good-bye, the DJ could only say thank you. The remaining calls that came the rest of the night were due to the power of one person's words. Call after call had the same message: love, caring, help one another. If you were listening an hour earlier, it was all about rage and anger, but after Kelley's call you might swear you had changed the channel.

I sat there listening for another 90 minutes or so before drifting off to sleep. Originally, I told Jen I would be in Oklahoma City for maybe two days. Now I'm thinking about heading home. If I didn't find him today, would I tomorrow? I was eager to get home. And when I do, I can develop the photos and find him in the crowd.

Just before dozing off for the night, the images of the offices came back into my mind. The destruction from across the blast zone may never leave my mind. The term "looks like a bomb went off" will forever have a new meaning. Maybe for the rest of my life. I also can't get past those pictures on the walls. How in the world is that possible? How could they have managed to stay hung in place? Well, there might be one idea. I'm glad I shared my discovery with that trooper. I might at some point think I dreamed the entire thing up if I hadn't.

There were picture of families, boyfriends, wives, family trips, hot air balloons, nature scenes, weddings. You name it. Photos of everything and anything scattered on the floor. Photos knocked off walls and desks lying under things and scattered around the office in general. Photos and other wall hangings busted up and left behind.

Very little survived inside those offices. Except for one thing. The same thing I asked that officer if he wanted to take pictures of for himself. Like me, he might want proof one day as he would no doubt try and explain what we had seen. They seemed to be in the exact spot in every office. As much as I tried, I couldn't find one busted frame or one piece of missing glass from any picture with him in it. Every single picture that survived that blast had the same man in it. That man was Jesus Christ.

1 Corinthians
Chapter 15 Verse 33

*Do not be misled: Bad company
corrupts good character.*

NIV

Chapter 10

Them Scientist Guys

November 23, 1996

"BY THE SWEAT OF YOUR BROW you will eat your food until you return to the ground, since from it you were taken; for dust you are and to dust you will return." A quote from the book of Genesis, 3:19. My grandmother was the first to read this to me, and more importantly, she taught me what this meant.

Sundays at my grandparents' house was family day. It always had been, long before my brothers and I moved in full time. As a kid, there was no way around it. After church we would do chores for an hour or two and afterward, if we weren't off to spend the afternoon fishing, it was Grandma's time with us. Now, that I have my own kids, nothing has changed.

On those nights we ate like kings at dinner. Grandma loved to cook, and it was normally the one day of the week we always had dessert. Grandma didn't hand out cash, didn't spoil us with gifts, but I will never forget those dinners. The big event for us, and what Grandma loved most, was having all four of her boys in one place all at the same time. Now she had a house full of grandkids *and* great grandkids.

The routine was always the same. Once the kitchen was clean, it was family time around the television. It wasn't an option either. During the fall it was football or a weekly program. Any other time of the year, we rented a movie. Years earlier, one night we had rented "Top Gun" starring Tom Cruise. Renting movies was the craze back in the late 80s.

Grandma and "Top Gun?" She hated it! She couldn't get into the powerful aircraft scenes and she didn't care for ninja motorcycles, the love story, or Goose's sense of humor. Watching her react to scenes throughout the movie was both painful and hilarious.

"Grandma...what's the deal? How could you not like this movie?" My brothers and I, and even Gramps beat her up pretty good about it. We were razzing her throughout the movie.

It was one of the greatest flicks of all time. After I saw it the first time, I was ready to join the Navy. Heck, Gramps was ready to drive me to the recruitment center the next day. My little brothers were making paper airplanes and were at war in the living room, but Grandma was coming from the bedroom with her Bible.

"Seriously, Grandma?" I said.

I was thinking how in the world could "Top Gun" turn into a Bible lesson. Before she even got into it, I was racking my brain. Not one scene of nudity. Not one blood and guts shootout. Nothing that should have warranted a chat about God and the good book.

"Do you know what I heard about that Tom guy?" Grandma said.

"Ah yeah, a lot. Which part about him or what story are you asking about?" I said.

"He's one of them scientist guys."

"What?" I asked a little confused.

"One of the scientist guys who don't believe in Jesus Christ. He's entitled to believe in what he wants but has got no business telling me that Jesus Christ didn't live."

"Did he really tell you that? You, that is?"

"Nope, didn't have to. I saw some TV show a week or so ago when he had made a comment about it. When you're talking poorly about Jesus, you might as well be talking bad about one of my boys."

She had me look up what Scientology meant.

Scientology is a set of beliefs and ideas written by founder L. Ron Hubbard. Scientology is described as the study and understanding of the spirit in relationship to itself, others, and all of life. One purpose of Scientology, as stated by the Church of Scientology, is to become certain of one's spiritual existence and one's relationship to God, or the "Supreme Being." One belief of Scientology is that a human is an immortal alien, i.e. extraterrestrial, spiritual being, termed a "thetan" that is trapped on earth in a physical body. Hubbard described these "thetans" in a "Space Opera" cosmogony. The thetan has had innumerable past lives, and it is accepted in Scientology that lives preceding the thetan's arrival on earth lived in extraterrestrial cultures. Descriptions of these space opera incidents are seen as true events by Scientologists.

Scientologist believe an individual should discover for himself/herself that Scientology works by personally applying its principles and observing or experiencing desirable results. Scientology claims that its practices provide methods by which a person can achieve greater spiritual awareness. Two primary methods of increasing spiritual awareness are referred to in Scientology as Auditing and Training. Within Scientology, advancement from level to level is often called a Bride to Freedom. Scientologist believe that a series of events occurred before life on earth. Scientologist also believe that humans have hidden abilities which can be unlocked.

"Absolute bunch of beans," Grandma said once I was finished reading it.

I have always believed in Jesus Christ. For me and my family, there was no question about it. However, I also always have believed that I'm not the smartest guy in the world. I've always wanted people to respect me for my faith. To get that respect though, you have to give it. I've run across many people who have different ideas: A Scientologist, Buddhist, and Taoist, whatever. Only one thing is certain: all kinds of different ideas are out there.

Grandma pulled us three boys together right then and there and told us all I ever needed to know about God vs. Scientology. For a gal who never graduated high school, what I was about to hear blew me away.

"How old do you think the oldest bible is?" She asked me.

"Thousands of years?" I said.

"James David...answer me honestly!"

Grams only addressed me or my brothers with middle names when she wanted serious answers. Both of my brothers just sat there. As usual, being the oldest meant I would be taking the heat in just about every conversation. No matter the subject, if grandma was speaking it was most likely directed my way and everyone knew better than to mingle mid-sentence with Grandma.

"Well, Jimmy?"

"I don't know...maybe since Jesus was alive?"

"Close. They have some printed versions that are several hundred years old. That's when many of the bibles started to appear with the different books all bound together to make up the bible as we know it today. Not all that long ago is when they appeared together collectively. The process of printing and binding books was a relatively new idea. The Bible was one of the first, but the different books or written words are, in some cases, thousands of years old."

"Okay... so how does Tom Cruise have anything to do with books and publications from hundreds of years ago?" I asked.

"Well, what do them scientists tell you? Something else other than Jesus Christ is in charge of your life. Or better yet, they try and tell you that something else other than God created us. I can prove that they are wrong, and the proof is right here in this book."

"Okay... how?" I asked.

"Well boys, some of the oldest scriptures you will find in the Bible were put together and are still found in museums and churches all around the world today. Some places in Europe have some of the first bound together books that are almost 1,200 years old. Now they aren't the same style as you see toady, but that's when "the Bible" started coming together. One of the early copies was the King James Bible. The words and teachings in it are copied from scrolls hidden away in sacred places all over the world. They say that over the years the Bible has been told and retold, written and re-written, in every single language, culture, and country in just about every square mile that this planet has to offer. And you know what? It has never changed! You three boys can't keep straight which one of you left the toilet seat up from day to day. How is it possible that a different version of the Bible hasn't popped up once...ever? But that's not the point I'm trying to make. Tom Cruise and his scientist group..."

"Scientologist...Grandma!" I'd try and correct her.

"Yes, them Scientologist never read the book of Genesis I bet you. All the answers you ever need about proof is right there. From dust we are, and to the dust we shall return. You know what that means boys?"

All of us froze. Gramps, me, and my brothers were still because we didn't want to miss what she was about to say next.

"Them Scientologist and other non-God believing folk all seem to forget that science, in the sense that we know it as, wasn't around hundreds of years ago. Genesis was written thousands of years ago. "From the dust we are, and the dust we shall return." Genesis 3:19. No matter how good science ever gets, it can't stop us from dying and turning to dust. Even the best scientist in the world will tell you that we are conceived from nothing. These scientists are working themselves stupid trying to prove that our God doesn't exist."

Again, we all sat there motionless and without words.

"So you boys tell me something. Them scientists will tell you that man created God. Don't they? Or did God create them scientists? Personally, I'll bet one day long after I'm dead and gone that all they will be able to prove is that the exact words from the Bible are nothing but the truth."

I'll remember those nights forever. Some of the best lessons I've ever learned, some of the best stories I've ever heard, were around that dinner table or in front of that television. My own kids are too young to fully enjoy or reflect on it, but those days, specifically those Sundays growing up, were the best.

Grandma ended up making it to 81 years old. She had been in hospice for eight months. A little longer than most patients typically stay. About seven years ago she was diagnosed with COPD. A lung disease that makes breathing, much less living, hard to imagine. If she wasn't so stubborn, I'm sure she would have been gone years before. She was always tough as nails.

The winter she died was the last time we spoke. Other than slowing down, she never really changed. Even though we didn't talk about it, she knew for years what I'd been up to. She never asked about how, or why, but she knew. We hadn't spent as much time together as Gramps and I had, but each time we did there wasn't a wasted minute. Over the last several years when we did chat, she began to speak less and listen more. Another great lesson. She'd tell me all the time that we have two ears and only one mouth. She didn't know everything, but she knew enough to have a good life.

She knew about the struggles between Jen and me. She had made a comment when we were dating about how finding your soulmate was tough and keeping your mate was even tougher. It was another comment Grandma made that was altogether too true.

Christmas of 2003 was the last good conversation I had with her. It was a day or two after Christmas and we spoke about simple things; family mostly. We spoke briefly about meals, what to eat, and better yet, what not to eat. Grandma was always wanting to make sure her family was not only fed, but properly fed at that. It wasn't my diet or food that I remember most about that conversation. Rather, before I left her side that night, she said one thing about my obsession that I'll always cherish.

For a woman that old, that tired, and having so much wisdom hearing her say, "James… I am rooting for you," was something I needed to hear. Marriage was tough and raising kids is even tougher. Having jobs not pan out and money issues can tear a man apart. Having her understand what I was going through made her death even harder on me.

"Thanks, Grandma. I know you understand. You might be the only one who knows all the grief and crap I deal with day in and day out. Sometimes I…."

She cut me off, "No, Jim…I am rooting for you, and you know exactly what I'm talking about."

For a brief moment, I wasn't sure what she was referring to, but before I could speak, she would finish.

"Jim, I hope you understand what you're doing. I hope you know it scares your family. Chasing after "him," to what end? That scares people. Not just because some folks might not see the reason, doesn't mean that your grandfather and I don't. It scares me, only because you are running after a man, or something, that could hurt you."

She stopped for a moment and I grabbed her hand and looked her square in the eyes. "Grandma, know this, I'll find him. I don't know what I'm going to do once I do find him, but I promise you that I will find him!"

With a smile on her lips and light tears in her eyes, she looked right at me and said, "Jimmy, your enthusiasm is what I'll miss the most. When you do find him, give him a little message for me will you? Tell that jackass your granny said all kinds of nice things about what he could go do with himself."

We both chuckled, I kissed her forehead and left for the day.

When it comes down to it, I've been a blessed man. Some would say my childhood was a little tested after the death of my parents, but really, death hasn't paid me another visit since. Others around me can't say that. It seems like every year since that day in the hills way back then, someone along my path has had to deal with death. It might be a co-worker's sibling, the neighbor's parents, or an old pal's boss. I didn't know it this morning, but death would be calling on me again that evening.

Death comes to us all at some point. Back on that dirt road when it first came to me, I thought that might be the worst I could ever feel. I've become a self-proclaimed expert in dealing with death. Most of the journeys I've been on have involved death in great numbers. Jennifer called and gave me the news. My grandmother had finally passed.

He had nothing to do with Grandma dying. I can guarantee you that. Even that coward knew not to mess with Grandma. From birth, she was always a mouthful. For 81 years she spoke her mind and didn't care who knew it. Grandma was born somewhere in northern Texas and was feisty and full of energy until her final days. Even when she was diagnosed with chronic obstructive pulmonary disease, they'd said it was in the advanced stages and she would probably be gone within a year, but she made it seven more. I'll remember her forever. The Bible says honoring thy parents is the best way for a long life. Well, if that's the case, I might just live another 100-plus years.

Proverbs
Chapter 3 Verse 6

In all your ways submit to him,
and he will make your paths straight.

NIV

Chapter 11

Storm Chasing

August 2005

A GREAT MANY THINGS HAVE HAPPENED the last several years. As hard as I've tried, quitting this addiction, this desire to find "him" or addiction that I have is more challenging that anything I've ever dealt with. I'm not sure why, but the need to succeed, or rather complete this task has for the most part, gotten the better of me.

I had it under control for a while until that school shooting at Columbine in Colorado fed the urge again. Maybe because of the kids involved. I'm not really sure why, but I am a father so that one hurt a lot. Or rather, it upset me enough to get back at it. I didn't know then, but slipping back into this need could be fueled by the slightest thought, or in that case, the quickest of trips.

The worst in the past several years though, was 9/11. Not just for what it was, but what that day did to me. And more importantly, what it did to my family. That just about sent Jen over the edge. I foolishly spent nine days away from her and the kids looking for "him." The end product was a depleted bank account, another lost job, and time away from her that I could never earn back.

The first night in my new apartment was really hard. No other way to put it. I would probably have a few more less-than-pleasant words about it if it wasn't for the fact that the next day, Saturday morning, sucked even more. I woke up on a mattress that I'd picked up at a garage sale. It was flat without a bounce and was only $25. I needed a bed. Sold! Friday night I slept on it without so much asa single sheet and I used a jacket for a blanket. Saturday morning, I took my first shower in my new place without a shower curtain. I hadn't thought about it until I had already been in the shower for ten minutes, but that's also when I realized I didn't have a towel. I left the bathroom dripping wet to dig through boxes searching for a sweatshirt to dry off with. The first 24 hours in my new place was off to a rough start.

Jen and I had finally separated. She'd had enough and I knew I wasn't being a good husband. Divorce, unfortunately was right around the corner. Over the last several years, what was an argument had turned into daily fighting. Even the smallest things that were cute years earlier were drawn out daily fights. Over the past couple of years, Jen grew tired of the "Jim Chasing satan: World Tour." I can't blame her; I question myself about what I'm doing more and more every day.

That winter, we did the best we could to fake it through the holidays. No sense crapping on the kids' plans with Santa Clause. I had stayed with Gramps until I found my new place. We gave the kids some excuse about Gramps being ill, and I was staying to help out. It worked...probably too well. After Christmas though, we decided it would be best to live apart. Done correctly, we could raise the kids in two homes. Divorce was no longer a maybe, but was coming to a courtroom later that summer.

Waking up that first morning in my new place, I realized that I really had to lean on some friends to help piece together a place to live. I'll never be able to repay what some pals did for me. I left everything except one TV and my personal items with Jen and the kids. I didn't need a lot. I've always shook my head in disgust hearing about divorces gone wrong. Ex-wives selling power tools in a garage sale for a buck a piece, ex-husbands washing wedding dresses with red socks. Both of them threatening to literally chainsaw couches in half. All the while, little Susie would be standing right there wondering why her parents didn't love each other. Divorce is tough, but you don't have to be an idiot.

It was early February of 2003 and the restaurant wasn't doing so well. The management's attitude toward me was running thin due to all of my last-minute trips. Jen knew what I was up to, but my employees didn't. I just kept making up stories to get out of work when I needed to travel. Over the past several years, I've been all over the country. Looking for "him" and following any "accident." There was that bad one outside of Houston. A mother of five who had killed her own children. I was sure "he" would be there. I went to any plane crash that took even a single life. Floods, earthquakes, and even a couple car crashes that were so bad, the National Transportation Safety Board got involved. Never once did I find "him," but I wasn't going to fail from a lack of trying.

As I was adjusting to life on my own, I didn't expect for "him" to visit when he did. My plan was to get on with life. Get some stability with a job. Build a home for the kids. Who knows, maybe find another lady? I even joined a gym to get back in shape. I had no plans to get back on the road. It was February 20th when "he" had made a visit to a night club in Rhode Island and claimed 100 victims in one of the worst fires in U.S. history.

Rhode Island was about a thousand miles from my new apartment. I could drive that blind folded. Round trip, it would probably run about $120 in gas. I had only about a hundred dollars in my account at the time, but I'd figure something out. As for my new boss, I'd tell him my brother was in trouble and blah, blah, blah. It worked before; why not start off this new job lying again? But the trouble with this trip was that my daughter's first basketball game was two nights away. I couldn't miss it.

I spent the entire day on the 21st working on a plan. I'd already told everyone at the restaurant that I might have to leave town. I borrowed $40 from an old friend for gas money. The weather, although cold, was no problem. It would be open highways from home to Rhode Island. Every angle that I had to get around was almost too easy. Except for the basketball game.

As much as I struggled with it, I finally decided it might be best not to drive to Rhode Island. My bank account needed the funds to stay put, my new boss needed the work done, and my daughter would really appreciate me being at her game. But the best reason for not going wasn't discovered until I actually was inside the gym and noticed the look on Jen's face when I walked through the door. That look made staying home all the more worthwhile.

When we were face to face, Jen sarcastically asked, "I thought for sure you would be in Rhode Island."

"Obviously not. She has a game tonight," I replied pointing a finger and waving to our daughter.

Another crack from Jen came my way, "Aren't you afraid you might miss "him"?

"Nope. I saw him just this morning. He visited the hell hole I call an apartment."

It wasn't all Jen's fault, and I guess I had some wisecracks coming. The divorce wasn't only because of my doing, I accept a large part of it as my fault. The hell of building a life again and living alone was an experience God warned us about. I think it's in the book of Malachi, 2:15 that God says he "hates divorce." When I first heard that, I wasn't sure what it meant, but I understand now.

The first time I heard that story was several years ago. As a teenager, living with my grandparents and sitting in church, we heard a sermon on the issue of divorce. When my parents died, they had never been with anyone but each other; my grandparents made it 50-plus years together. Divorce wasn't a part of my life, so paying attention to the subject in my mind wasn't necessary. Why God hates divorce. I didn't care back then, but it has my full attention now.

What a pain in the butt. Everything about a divorce sucks. Thinking about it, I can't put an honest answer or idea of what makes a divorce worth it. Jen has been and always probably will be a great woman, and she still is as beautiful as ever. I've spent plenty of time thinking about the pros and cons and have really come up with nothing. Nothing worth debating that is.

God hates divorce for two reasons. The first is simply when you get married and then one day decide to divorce, you are breaking your word with God. Anyone who gets married in a Christian setting makes the same promises. In sickness and in health. For richer or poor. Till death do us part. We swear in front of God, family, and friends that this one is it. She's the one, God. I swear.

The other reason is because divorce destroys relationships. Going through it, the outcome wasn't anything I considered prior, but what happens to all those joint friends and families we hung out with? Jen had some really cool friends with spouses that I really enjoyed spending time with. Now what? All of them are gone from my life. I never really cared for her mother, but I thought her father and brothers were the coolest guys in the world. Now they are gone. My grandfather actually really liked Jen and now what? Every relationship gone. Even people outside our friends and family circles. Family night at school will forever be different, the insurance agent who we played softball with, heck, even he was put in a tough spot. And finally, the bank. Although society has loosened its disapproval on divorce, the bank sure hasn't. Try getting a loan to buy a bicycle now. Once again, relationship terminated. It's safe to say that I understand clearly why God hates divorce.

Perhaps one thing that I benefited from our divorce was the amount of time I now spend reading. I can't afford cable, and the amount of stuff being published on-line is almost overwhelming. I can't help but wonder how magazines and newspapers will survive the internet age. I've purchased more books than ever before just to fill my alone time. I recently picked up a book called *The Purpose Driven Life*. It was a great book that was easy to read and got me thinking about a variety of things.

I thought mostly about my time with my family, my kids, grandparents, and brothers. Is there really anything more important in life? Thinking back while we were married, I often thought about the amount of parenting Jen was doing by herself. How unfair to her and the kids. When I was at home, not at work or on the road, I was either digging through newspapers or my photographs looking for "him." Some nights, I was spending three or four hours looking at pictures and news clips. It only got worse with the internet's availability. My office at home was littered with photos, newspaper clippings, and maps of where I've been and where I might be going next.

Odd the things that you do. I can't tell anyone how my kids' rooms are decorated, but I could tell you the exact distance it was from my driveway to a casualty somewhere in the U.S. How depressing that makes me feel.

I also thought recently about how much time Jen and I spent in church with or without the kids. For several years, Christmas and Easter were about it. We did occasionally slip in a few Sunday mornings and had the kids go to Sunday school. It's funny; we have our kids at school without fail Monday through Friday at 8:30 in the morning until 4:00 in the afternoon. If our kids are struggling in a subject, we will find the time and money for extra help. Sunday school though? It lasts an hour or so once a week and getting them there was done only a handful of times. Looking back, church was always in my heart, but my mind was always doing other things.

About six months after that first crappy Saturday, I am again sitting in bed on yet another weekend morning bored, lonely, unmotivated, and not feeling all that great about life. Alone physically, spiritually, and emotionally. All of it. I might even say I'm bordering on depression. I wake up in my empty apartment to silence. No kids running around, no TV blaring from the other room, nobody else in the shower. Nada. Zilch. It's dead silent.

As I lay in bed, I still have visions of seeing "him." Running "him" down, maybe even assaulting "him." How great it would be to sucker punch "him" in the mouth? That vision makes me laugh. I'd probably get my ass kicked, but I could imagine God sitting up in heaven with Jesus and all the crew looking down and watching the fist fight break out. I can almost picture Jesus and one of his pals making side bets on how long I'd last. However, in reality, my system sucks. Parts of my entire life suck. I'm out of shape, divorced, and broke. I won't catch "him" while running on empty in life like I am. I really need to get back on top of a lot of things. Maybe I will start by helping coach one of the kid's sports teams. Maybe do some volunteering, get more active in a church, or pay some bills before they are past due for a change.

The best thing I can do for my kids is lead by example. That, and of course a right hook to you know who, might be cool. Saturday morning, August 20th started off the same as most of my Saturdays. Not much going on with not much planned for the rest of the day. I lay in bed wide awake and depressed. No idea of what, when, why, how, or where life was going to happen for me. I finally succumed to cable, so I grabbed the remote and flipped on the TV searching for something worth watching. Oddly, the first channel I went to was a movie channel playing the hit movie, "Forrest Gump."

The movie was more than half over at the point I tuned in. Forrest had just had "his Jenny" leave him again. As he sat there alone with nothing to do, probably more than confused about the relationship mess he was in, Forrest decided to go on a little run. Why not, I thought?

For the past several years I hadn't seen the inside of a gym. Becoming out of shape was an understatement. For such an athletic kid growing up, I haven't done anything active in a long time. Maybe Forrest was on to something. A Saturday morning run sounded like the perfect plan.

Unlike Forest, I couldn't make it across the country and back again. Heck, I was so out of shape I couldn't make it out of the apartment complex before almost having a heart attack. Still, I got out of the house and did both a little running and a lot of walking. While doing so, I also did some thinking. I thought about my life plan and how to get there.

As a bonus, in the middle of my run, or I should say my walk, I ran by this church I had been eyeing as a place I'd like to visit. Southeast Christian. On the marquee out front it read: Saturday evening service was 5:00-6:00 p.m. Well this day is shaping up, I thought. If I don't die from running for the first time in five years, I might just make an appearance.

I returned home after about an hour, and quickly showered. I thought about catching up on some news via the internet. I had something to do at 5:00 now, so I had several hours to catch up on events and who knows, maybe get lucky and spot "him" online somewhere. I routinely hit *The USA Today, The New York Times,* and my local papers every day. *The USA Today* and *New York Times* covered stories coast to coast. Not to mention both had great articles and photos. Who knows? I could get lucky, so I never missed a day.

Both newspapers had the same leads on the front page. Something about the Jewish settlers being removed from the Gaza Strip and the other big story was about a hurricane. It was only a tropical storm at the time. However, it would become Hurricane Katrina and it was bearing in on the southern United

States' coast. I read both articles, but I didn't have a stake in either place so neither one got much of my attention. At least that's what I thought until I sat through my first church service in only God knows how long.

Southeast Christian's Saturday evening service worked well with my typical non-eventful Saturdays. And as an added bonus, I could sleep in on Sunday. The pastor was finishing a three-week series on storms. The actual series was called "Storm Chasing." A little odd having read in detail hours earlier about the hell heading toward the Gulf Coast. This is where they were in the series.

From the program I read that week one was a storm series sermon called "Sin-full Storms." Devoted to educating and detouring us around and through the storms in our lives brought upon us by nothing other than sin. Thinking about it, what other thing has done more damage to a life than when sin has been in the mix?

The next week was named "Stupidity Storms." The things you do in your life that creates issues caused by stupid things. Maybe sleeping in and needing to speed to that meeting caused you to get a speeding ticket? Thus, in turn causes a financial hardship. Those issues in life are all avoidable and normally only caused by stupid errors.

It would be fair to say, the majority of my issues in life are a perfect 50/50 split between sin and stupidity. I'd probably guess the same amount for most people I know. And for the last storm in this series? Well, once I heard the pastor say the words, it almost completed that heart attack from my run earlier in the day. The storms may not be in your control, you may never see them coming, but the storms that do the most damage are the storms caused by satan: "satan storms!"

"What the...?" was my first reaction.

I couldn't really believe this was being preached. *Are you serious*, I asked myself at least a half dozen times? I haven't been to church in who knows how long. I haven't run in even longer and only came to church as a result of running.

The movie I watched today, "Forrest Gump," his turning point in life was a storm. Aboard the boat he named *Jenny*, he and Sargeant Dan had a run in with a little storm of their own. The cover story on every paper in America today is about hurricane Katrina! As I sit there in church in complete disbelieve, I started to connect the dots from just today alone. Was all this really by chance? Was this all just by coincidence? There is no possible way all of this was random.

Oh yeah, you bet your butt. I truly believe God is talking. I've begged for his direction, always looking for signs and questioned myself no less than a hundred times about my doings. I prayed nonstop for an answer and for help along the way. Seems like New Orleans is the path for Katrina. So be it! Even though they are preparing for a mass evacuation, tomorrow I will prepare for my arrival.

Romans
Chapter 8 Verse 18

I consider that our present sufferings are not worth comparing with the glory that will be revealed in us.

NIV

Chapter 12

Signs

August 2005

I FLAT OUT TOLD JENNIFER, "I was going."

Luckily it was her weekend with the kids. I was already packed when I approached her with it.. I didn't lie about it or BS her this time. I told her about my entire day on Saturday: church, Katrina, everything. Heck, we even joked about "Forest Gump." As we spoke Sunday morning about me going, I'd thought previously to the conversation and thought I'd need to be prepared for some kind of push back. Some kind of heat or complaint from her. As it turned out, Jen was cool as ever and said, "Good luck, Jim. Be safe."

My boss was a different story. We were right in the middle of a sizable project. I thought it was best not to lie to him, but what could I do? After all, following the message I received from going to church yesterday, I couldn't ignore the signs. I wasn't about to tell him I was heading south to find the devil. So, I told him I was heading south to help the rescue efforts and the Red Cross. I was going to find a shelter and dig in. My patriotic duties obligated me, I told him. Or some kind of baloney like that. He was okay with the idea but not with the timing. He had served in Vietnam and understood the bold red, white, and blue passion. But he also understood that things needed to happen quickly on our project. So quick that any loss of manpower that week could jeopardize not only this project but his company in general. I had a choice, be at work all week, or hope that my patriotic duties could land me another job. Well, the sign I received was from God, and I knew it. I was out of a job when I found this one and I guess I'll be looking again next week when I get back home.

After I hung up the phone with him, and having his ultimatum, I made my decision. I never made it back to work for him again.

Before I left home, I still had to choose where to go. This was a monster of a storm and if I wanted any chance of finding "him" I would have to be in the right place. I spent the rest of the day reviewing maps, watching updates on TV, and making my game plan.

I've never been to Panama City or Pensacola. Those parts of Florida were under warning, but the storm seemed to be heading west. I had been to Grayton Beach, a state park in Florida between the two cities, when I was a kid. We had a great time there fishing, but for some reason I just didn't think that seemed like a place "he" would be heading. Too clean, too nice of people, and too many palm trees. Florida was off the list.

It was also reported that Houston might be a landing zone. Or even south of there in Corpus Christi, Texas. I drove through Corpus Christi once on a trip to South Padre Island, back in high school when a bunch of buddies and I road tripped for spring break. That was a fun week except for that drive. No way was I driving that far again and in a storm to boot.

The last update I heard before heading out was that Katrina was now a full-on hurricane. I didn't leave until around noon. The radio and TV stations were non-stop tracking this beast. The National Weather Service rated this storm as an F5, the most powerful of storms. Wind speeds in a F5 can reach over 200 miles per hour. One TV weather anchor mentioned that a typical 747 aircraft weighs over 200,000 pounds and it only needs about 140 miles per hour to reach flight. I think everyone listening understood that an F5 hurricane was a serious deal.

New Orleans and the surrounding area seemed like the target. All the weather forecasters and other experts were zeroing in on New Orleans as being the storm's major target. The time of landing was updated constantly. Of course, all the experts were making predictions on its destruction. Water levels from the rain alone could set records. Ocean surges were predicted to be high as well. If "he" was making an appearance, this is where "he" would be heading. Now, just where in New Orleans should I go?

The entire drive to New Orleans was just short of 600 miles. As I got closer to the city, the roads opened up nicely. Southbound, that is. Northbound was altogether different. In some spots, the highways looked like a scene from a movie. Two and three lane roads with literally an entire city worth of people packed in any vehicle that could move. I blew by them all heading toward the city at 70 miles per hour. The day before Katrina's landing, the weather was still decent. Wind and moisture were definitely present, but things were changing by the hour.

I thought while driving that I've watched shows on TV about storm chasers. You know, those idiots following tornadoes all over God's creation. I've wondered why in the world would anyone do that? Well, I guess I am now officially a part of that club.

For the most part, the weather wasn't much of an issue. At least not during the early part of the day. When I left Kentucky that morning heading south, the skyline was red. Almost a blood red with lots of purples and blues mixed in. Very cool looking, but also very ominous. You could see the sun fighting its way through, but old yeller would lose that battle the farther I drove into Mississippi. It reminded me of something my grandfather told me about during his service in the Navy.

"Red sky at night...a sailors delight. Red sky in morning, sailors take warning!" A saying passed down through ship captains everywhere. Navy, Coast Guard, commercial, or private boat captains and crew all subscribed to the same idea. My entire life, Gramps was always rambling about the good ole' days and these little saying he picked up in the Navy never altered. Oddly how accurate they were as well. If the red sky in the morning belief held true, all hell was coming this direction.

As I drove closer toward the city, between every song on the radio were commercials and public service announcements. The PSA's went on and on. Go here, do this, not that, buy this, get one of these. The main message? If able, get out of New Orleans ASAP.

One station quit airing songs and only broadcast emergency notices. I was probably about an hour or so outside the city, sitting idle in a little town called Picayune. Getting into New Orleans was starting to become a hassle. The forced evacuations from the coming storm closed streets everywhere. The number of people leaving the area was hard to imagine.

Parts of highway I-10 were closing. Of course, every time I was warned off by police, I lied about why I needed to move forward. As long as there was no water, I had work to do in New Orleans. It's a major interstate that wraps around Pontchartrian, a massive lake just inland. The lake looks as big as an ocean and as hard as I tried, I ended up having to drive around it.

I spent way more time than planned trying to get into the city. The weather was getting worse and it was getting dark. A few times I had to stop on the side of a road to get my direction straight. I'm not normally directionally challenged and don't struggle for where I'm going, but this storm seamed to create struggles even from my front seat on where I was going. I had no idea where I was, but it didn't matter. I got very lucky in the parking lot of a grocery store called Leblanc's.

"Are you Bill?" The voice came from behind me in a little bus rolling up beside me.

"No, I am not. Can I help you?" I said.

"Not unless you're heading into New Orleans," the stranger said.

"Well actually, I am heading into New Orleans," I replied.

"You're kidding me? I noticed the truck and thought you might be Bill. Don't know him directly, but I'm just rounding up whoever I can to help. I have a trailer that needs to get into the city, and this bus can't pull it. I have a truck over there already hooked up. You can drive that or yours, I don't care, but we gotta roll."

And just like that, I was following this random guy, Cory Sanders was his name, into New Orleans. Apparently, the mandatory evacuations have a deadline of 6:00 p.m. He had some pump part that had to get to a public service building. Cory was driving a little bus filled with all kinds of tools. Apparently, he does contract work, both private and commercial in the city. I didn't care, he needed a driver and I needed an escort into the city. I left my truck in the parking lot and we were off to New Orleans. Absolutely perfect. Or so I thought.

The drive took roughly two hours, twice as long as normal. We went through more side streets and alley ways that I knew for sure weren't roads. I mean some of them may have been on a map at some point, but the others I couldn't seem to find them on any map. The wind and rain were intensifying each minute. I could tell something bad was heading to New Orleans.

As it turned out, we dropped off his equipment and vehicles about two miles from downtown. He was already dressed and packed for the trip. Cory had thought it might be a day or two. I left the house in Kentucky ready. Ready for what though? I knew all along the Superdome was going to house anyone who couldn't get out of town. I also knew the convention center was an option, but the Superdome sounded more exciting. I've never been inside of one before.

I made it to the dome late but easily. I think the majority of people went in through the main entrance, but we entered through a group of doors by the large vehicle entrances. There were a lot of people on the concourses wrapping around the playing field. They were running around trying to organize and set up their "space" for the night. The number of people on the field shocked me. I would guess about 20 thousand. I didn't have a sleeping bag and any cots brought in from the city were already taken up, but I've been through worse sleeping situations than this. At least, that's what I thought at 10 p.m.

***

THAT WAS THE LONGEST 24 HOURS OF MY LIFE. As the night became morning, I never closed an eyelid. If it wasn't the winds roaring outside it was the noise inside that sounded nothing short of a rock concert with a handful of idiots that made everyone uncomfortable. Before I was allowed into the dome, I was searched for drugs and alcohol. They also asked if I had a gun. Weapons were not permitted inside the dome. Good thing because I may have used it.

All night there was screaming and crying from every direction. The wind, although incredibly loud, actually helped to drown out the human voices. Idiot after idiot wandering around almost looking for trouble. Many trying to steal whatever you might not be using or tending to. They were everywhere and looked like gang members from the movies with pants dropped halfway down their butts. It was about six in the morning when all hell broke loose outside. Two of these assholes stood up, dropped their pants, and pissed on the seats in front of them. I eye-balled the idiots and the next thing I know they were approaching me. I looked them right in the eyes almost daring them to start something. Was I scared? Hell yes, but I wasn't about to look weak while trying to defend all the helpless people around us. They scuffed some harsh words and walked away.

The amount of people desperately trying to find comfort was rapidly deteriorating. The nerves of most everyone were absolutely shot. Long before 9 a.m. local time, I had the feeling that I was a rat inside of a trap. Things went from bad to worse. What in the HELL am I doing here? I thought to myself.

You could see parts of the roof coming apart and light was coming in from outside. I wouldn't have believed it if it wasn't for the water pouring in. What was already a bad situation in the outlying areas of the dome was now hitting the inside surface. I was still in the same section of seats in the lower bowl. People were running around screaming that the roof was falling. I'll admit, I also started to panic.

Roughly 24 hours ago, I had an idea that riding out the hurricane inside the Superdome sounded exciting. The same feeling you get before going into a haunted house. Spooky, I thought. Maybe we'll all get scared and hold hands and probably laugh when it's all done. There are 20,000 people in this building. Men, woman, and children of every age and every race with people from several parts of the world. Nobody had laughed about anything long before setting foot in this hell hole. If I survive this one day, I'll tell anyone who will listen about this being the worst day of my life, besides my parents' death, of course.

The storm outside did not quit. I was within earshot of a couple who had been through Hurricane George. He was an older gentleman with his wife. He looked at her at one point and said "Honey, this isn't no Hurricane George. We're in trouble!"

It never dawned on me that my cell phone wouldn't work. I had left my cooler with water back in my truck. I had a bag with one change of clothes, my camera, and that's it. I thought that right after the hurricane, I and the others stuck here would wander outside and maybe grab a cocktail at the first watering hole on Bourbon Street. Driving into New Orleans yesterday was single-handedly the absolute dumbest thing I have ever done.

The first 24 hours in the dome was completely nuts. Hysteria was everywhere. Because of the storm, I expected people to be scared and I expected some people to say and do some dumb things. But although this really wasn't a place I'd like to be right now, I thought how tomorrow would bring an end to this madness.

On Tuesday I was awakened by more screaming. Next to me were two young girls by themselves. They attended Tulane University and were visiting some guys, maybe a boyfriend, but Sunday morning, he and his friends left them alone in his apartment. They did not return. Nice! The two girls were scared out of their minds and had done more crying than talking.

Directly behind me and to my left were a few older ladies. Four very talkative locals, maybe even native to the area. They came prepared. They had purses bigger than most duffle bags and every once in a while, they would reach in and come out with trial mix or other snacks. They had pillows and some blankets.

There were several young kids in the area as well. A couple with what might be a mother and a father. Disturbingly though, there were several kids who appear to be with just their moms. No adult male role model, those moms and kids on their own. The only smile I've seen in the past day or so was from a couple of those kids, I'm sure because they don't know the danger in the storm outside.

All the while, as I sat in the Superdome, I searched for "him." Coming here yesterday, I never really thought about "him" making an appearance in the dome. At the time, the dome was just going to house me for the night. But now, this could be the perfect place to run into "him." Although I haven't been walking around looking, I've looked at almost everyone in this building. Those around me, those walking by, pretty much anyone I could eyeball. However, no luck. Yet.

You can tell people are settling into their areas. Only 24 hours ago, families were sitting with one another. Now people are massing together in large groups. The storm outside appears to have left New Orleans. However, another storm was brewing or rather moved right into the superdome. If I had to do it over again, I might have very well taken my chances outside.

The staff and National Guard have been passing out small bits of food and water. That's been the extent of the luxury. I feel trapped like there is nowhere for me to move. I can't even stretch my legs. Mobs of punks and individual assholes are everywhere. The bathrooms are overflowing with sewage. The smell from 20,000 people who haven't showered in two or three days is pretty much unbearable.

The lights are barely on, so it's fairly dark. There is no air conditioning and you can tell the Louisiana summer heat and humidity are back outside. The Superdome is becoming more like an oven and less like a sporting facility. People are turning over vending machines trying to get food. We were told that the National Guard would be here tomorrow to start evacuating us to outlying areas.

They showed up the next day. However, they brought other people needing a place to stay. The population has now grown by another four or five thousand people in the last 12 hours and tempers were out of control. We have had a few guardsmen in our area for the entire day. Thank God! Keeping as friendly as possible with them, I found out some information that made me sick to my stomach.

Apparently the state and federal government have been haggling over who, what, where to send food, water, and supplies--48 hours of bullshit. The President was playing golf; the Governor was reacting to needs from a piece of scratch paper. The Saint's Football team could do better at drawing up plays in the dirt. Both the state and feds were winging this as they went along. We heard that a Pepsi bottling plant sent two tractor trailers full of water toward the city, but were turned away at a road block a few short miles away.

But that's not the worst. Apparently, the Coast Guard has been trying to fly in chopper supplies, too. Food, water, diapers, medicine, all kinds of goods. The choppers are turned away because they are being shot at.

"Shot at?" I asked angrily. "Why is anyone being shot at?"

The National Guardsman said, "Probably the same kind of people you see right over there." He pointed at three men. You can imagine the picture. Thugs, probably three gang members.

They were maybe 18-24 years of age. Just punk kids. All three without a top on and ball caps turned backwards. I guess losing your shirt and walking around with your pants hanging below your ass looks pretty cool. These were the same assholes who have been walking around just looking for trouble, looking for any fight they could start.

As the two guardsmen and I continued to talk, I overheard the four elderly women talking about a recipe one had gotten off a TV show. Something about a mixture of crackers, cheddar cheese, and broccoli. *Unreal,* I thought. Now that was funny. All hell breaking lose and these ladies are exchanging recipes. I guess they are too old, too tired, and really what can they do to improve their situation? I knew the minute they sat down that I liked them all.

I did get lucky when Osceola McGrady came in and sat just to the right of my two chairs during the night. An older lady, probably in her late 70s, maybe early 80s. Little did I know when we said hello, that she'd tell me something about "him" that I had never thought about before. She was very sweet, kind, and soft spoken and said she had lived in the south her entire life.

Later that day, Osceola and I sat and chatted. The two college girls were still in front of us, both of them writing out what I swear were goodbye letters to their friends and families. Osceola talked a lot about God, so I had no doubt that she was a believer.

126

We chatted for about an hour just about our backgrounds before she mentioned something I had never heard before.

"You know this storm is God's wrath," she said with an eerie grin on her face.

"His wrath? Did we do something wrong?" I said almost jokingly.

"Have been for years, keeps getting worse, too."

"Why would you say that?" I was confused.

"Do you have your Bible?" she asked as she reached in her bag and grabbed an old brown Bible that I bet was almost as old as she was.

"Ah no, I left it at home," I said almost sheepishly. How ironic I thought that was. I go all over chasing the devil, but I don't even bring my Bible with me.

"Well Jim, that ain't doing you no good there. We'll just have to share mine," she said with a smile.

She gave me her Bible and said, "Now open that to Zechariah 12 and read me one to three."

In an instant I felt like a troubled schoolboy. I knew she meant no harm, but her look and tone was almost sarcastic and disappointed that not only did I not have a Bible with me, but that I didn't know what it was she was asking me to read. *Who carries a Bible with them anyway?* I thought.

It was obvious that she did. While digging through hers; it had more highlighter and pen marks then actual print. Osceola had used this book a lot. I began to read it aloud. The two girls turned around and listened to every word.

"Now Jim, you understand what that means, don't you?"

I nodded my head to indicate yes, but at the same time I asked if she could explain it a little better. Her Bible is a King James version. The same version I have at home. It's a little tough to read with older words and parables that are hard to follow. Anyway, she mapped it out and explained to us what it meant.

She went into detail and spoke about the blessing of Israel and how God has made it clear throughout the Bible that his people will be saved, and those who stand against them shall be punished.

"God's promise to his people. Them Jewish folk we ought not be messing with," she said.

"Messing with them? How are we messing with them?" I asked, confused.

"Read the daily paper, Jim. It's right there in black and white. The news reports on TV are no good."

"I have to tell you Osceola, I do read the paper. Several of them, usually every day. I've been reading them for years looking for someone. Nothing ever alarmed me about anyone messing around with Jewish people."

"When's the last time you read a paper?" she asked.

"This past Saturday. I read a couple papers. Actually, one of them had two stories on the front page that I do remember. One about this storm right now, and the others about Jewish settlers or something in the Gaza Strip."

"Oh really?" she replied with sarcasm.

"And what did you learn about the Jewish settlers?"

"To be honest, I scanned through it without giving it a second thought. How does that affect us over here? And how could something over there be causing this storm?"

Even though I eagerly awaited her response, ideas were starting to form in my head about the story. The story I didn't really read last Saturday. Could they be linked? The storms and Jewish settlers? Could the message I had heard in church not have been about finding "him" in this storm, but somewhere else?

She continued, "Do you have an idea how many times the U.S. government has tried to force themselves and our foreign agendas in Israel? And every time, we get our fannies tanned."

"Tanned? You mean spanked? Spanked by who?" I said completely perplexed.

"Well Jim, God. That's who. The Bible is the past, present, and future. In the book of Psalms, Acts, Ezekiel, Peter, Isaiah, and many others. Messages are also in the first and the last chapters: Genesis and Revelations. All of them speak of warnings."

I sat for a moment staring into her face. Grinning, almost beaming of light. She sat back and watched me react. The two girls never said a word. As I was trying to wrap my head around Osceola's comments, we were interrupted by one of the guards I was speaking with earlier in the day.

"We are leaving in 20 minutes. We are getting this group out." The guard said in a hushed voice.

He continued. "Don't tell a person. Not one single person, you understand me? We can't cause a riot here with people storming out in all directions. Small groups are all we can handle right now. We are already losing control. We can't babysit the situation any better than we currently are. You understand the circumstance? You are either going now or staying until later. You, the girls, and those older ladies--20 minutes, and we are gone. Got it?"

True military style. No talking about it, no negotiating, I was told where to be and that was final. Either be there, or stay behind in the hell we were sitting in. I sat there briefly thinking of the plan. The older ladies wouldn't move very fast, but the younger girls I knew, would move quickly. We could not draw attention to us. My plan was the bathroom.

I told each one of them quietly that we are leaving. Leaving from the dome, heading outside, and out of New Orleans. I explained it in the exact military fashion that it was explained to me. Move and move quietly, or we'll be left behind. I didn't have to repeat myself. All seven women wanted out.

The departure was actually the easiest part of the entire ordeal. One at a time, we started walking away from our seats like we were heading to the bathroom. Nothing that looked urgent to an outsider, but still, we moved quickly. Looking around as I was leaving, I did notice other small groups had also disappeared from where they were sitting. I never noticed. We obviously weren't the first group to leave.

Our group was nervous, but I guess when you have armed escorts that use locked back doors toward waiting boats and military transportation trucks you're in good hands. It took us five minutes from the time we left our seats to get outside. The first thing we all felt was the sun, heat, and humidity on our faces. What a great feeling. Normally, that time of year, that sensation might not have been pleasant. For anyone leaving the dome, by comparison, it was pure paradise.

Getting back to my truck took the better part of another day. Being transported out of New Orleans and seeing what the hurricane had done to that great city was hard to imagine much less describe. If you are a God fearing person, you'd use the words Apocliptic Event.

The entire drive home I spent listening to the radio thinking about missing "him." "He" *had* to have been down there. Again, as hard as I tried, I just couldn't find, much less see "him" anywhere. No way "he" would have missed that show. Perhaps "he" didn't make it to the dome. Perhaps "he" was the ring leader and I just missed "him."

Sooner or later though, I'll find "him."

Genesis
Chapter 12 Verse 2-3

I will make you into a great nation, and I will bless you; I will make your name great and you will be a blessing. I will bless those who bless you, and whoever curses you I will curse; and all the peoples on earth will be blessed through you.

NIV

Chapter 13

So Goes Israel,
So Goes the World

I ONCE READ WHERE A STORM'S NAME COMES FROM. Some think hurricane names are just random and are selected from a list of hated neighbors, ex's, or bullies from school. Maybe the person who picked Hurricane Andrew was about a kid that stole someone's lunch money. Maybe Hurricane Floyd was the name of a neighbor who had a dog that loved your prize-winning roses. And Katrina? I can only guess how badly that heart was broken.

Names for hurricanes are actually based on several factors. Really. What part of the world, what ocean, date lines, and so forth is only part of the process. Then there is this six-year list that cycles and rotates men and woman's names. After that, names are retired for "X" reasons and other names are chosen for a new list. You'd think picking a name would easier, but for storms, especially hurricanes, there is all kinds of scientific nonsense behind the process.

As I was planning how to get into New Orleans for Hurricane Katrina, I read something in the paper about the Jewish settlers being removed in the Gaza Strip. Not that I or anyone else I know really care, but the article's author researched both sides of the issue. It wasn't an American reporter who wrote the article, but it was picked up by *The USA Today*.

In his interview with one of the settlers, a quote was mentioned that for the life of me I can't get out of my head. "So goes Israel, so goes the world!"

He continued until he also referred to a piece of scripture that caught my eye. Zechariah 12: 1-3. "Thus declares the Lord who stretches out the heavens, lays the foundation of the earth, and forms the spirit of man within him. Behold, I am going to make Jerusalem a cup that causes reeling to all the peoples around; and when the siege is against Jerusalem, it will also be against Judah. It will come about in that day that I will make Jerusalem a heavy stone for all the peoples; all who lift it will be severely injured. And all the nations of the earth will be gathered against it."

Interesting, I thought. After 30 years Jewish settlers were forced to leave their occupied territories in mid-August of 2005. On the other side of the globe, America's largest and what would end up being one of the deadliest and most expensive hurricanes in history was about to hit. Both events literally happening at the same time. But this wasn't the first time this had happened either.

George Bush, the elder, attended the Madrid Peace Talks in 1991. In October, to be exact. It was called the *Land for Peace Deal*. Israel could gain peace with its neighbors by simply giving up land. Seems reasonable, but some would tell you that is exactly the opposite of God's plan. At the exact same time a storm developed off the coast of Nova Scotia. The storm moved over a thousand miles from east to west generating waves over one hundred feet tall. In *The USA Today* it was called the "perfect storm." And on the same front page was a story about the *Land for Peace Deal*.

In August of 1992, more peace talks moved to Washington DC and again, a storm of epic size and damage was coming. The

National Weather Service referred to Hurricane Andrew as a 25-30-mile-wide tornado with incredible winds. Again, on the front page of *The USA Today* read, "One Million Flee Andrew." Also sharing the front page was, "Mideast peace talks to resume with good hope." At the end of the day, Andrew hit the coast of Florida causing over 30 billion dollars in damage.

As I was reading about the odd timing of these events, I ran across this piece of scripture: Jeremiah 25:32. "Thus saith the Lord of hosts, Behold, evil shall go forth from nation to nation, and a great whirlwind shall be raised up from the coasts of the earth." As I continued my fact finding, the timing of these storms and worldly political events continued.

In early September of 1993 *The New York Times* had a few events posted right there on page one. One was about a joint Israel and PLO recognition. Something about an agreement to be signed in Washington. I didn't read much about it, but the other article was about yet another storm. Hurricane Emily hitting the Outer Banks. Again, happening at the same time.

January 16, 1994, President Bill Clinton was in Switzerland. Why he was there, I don't know, but his quote was, "Israel must make concessions that will NOT be politically popular by Israelites." Less than 24 hours later, a 6.9 magnitude earthquake hit the north-ridge of California.

March 1, 1997, Yasser Arafat was in Washington to meet with the United Nations. I didn't have the full article, but again *The New York Times* headline was about President Clinton rebuking Israel. The very next day, the largest recorded tornado on record would hit Texas, Oklahoma, Arkansas, Mississippi, Kentucky, Tennessee, and Ohio. It caused record flooding and damage. One governor described the damage as an "apocalyptic event never seen before." Maybe he was right; the National Weather Service said you might see this kind of storm once every 500 years.

In late January of 1998, the prime minister of Israel met with President Clinton to discuss the Land for Peace deals.

Of course, it didn't go as well as the President wished, and he publicly voiced his displeasure. Additionally, Clinton went so far as to cancel lunch plans with the prime minister. Later that afternoon, a certain famous sex scandal broke out about the President.

In late September of 1998, Yasser Arafat met with Madeleine Albright to again discuss Land for Peace deals. The U.S. government strongly encouraged Israel to surrender 13 percent of its land. They would meet in New York City and on the exact same day, Hurricane George would slam into the Gulf Coast with winds up to 175 miles per hour.

Just a few weeks later in mid-October, Arafat would meet the Israel's prime minister in Maryland for ten days. Ten days of talk about the Land for Peace *again*. Two days into the meeting, rain started in Texas and continued for over a week. Flooding hit parts of Texas like never before. The rains ironically concluded the same day that the Land for Peace meetings ended.

May 4, 1999, Arafat again pressured Israel for land and the exact same day, the most powerful tornado hit Oklahoma and Kansas. It was a collection of tornados including one with winds of 300 miles per hour. A different tornado in the area was said to be over a mile wide.

September 13, 1999. Again, the US was mingling in foreign affairs. It was the same story on front pages around the country. Our government, our President, Israel to deal. Same outcome, too. Halfway around the globe, a category five hurricane named Floyd with winds of 155 miles per hour slammed into the coast of the Carolinas. I guess you could say that this one wasn't that bad though. Only a little over a billion dollars in damage reported.

As hard as I tried, I couldn't find the devil anywhere in these articles. I never found "him" in New Orleans either. I've read until I can't take it anymore. If I happen to read something and notice anything peculiar so be it, but I'm done digging through everything written about death and destruction.

The media has a unique way of writing. Articles and stories written by those who write, for simply the love of writing, I seem to like more. You can just about hear the truth come right off the page. However, in some of those high-priced newspapers and magazines, the more I read, the more I wanna say "B.S." They seem to flip just about every story. What is good is evil. What is evil is good. What is right is wrong, and of course, what is wrong is right.

I'm not quite sure what to think of the odd timing of these events and many more like them. Of course the media will tell you, its global cooling like they did in the 70s. Then it was global warming. And now it's climate change. I don't know what to believe anymore. To be honest, if it's cold, I just grab a jacket.

I remember another idea back in Sunday School many years ago that might be as good as any with trying to explain these odd coincidences. Years and years ago, I had a Sunday School teacher who made it very clear. I haven't thought about it until recently, but the Jews are God's chosen people. We were told that God has love for all. Whites, Blacks, Latino's, Orientals, Arabs, and on, and on. He gave life to us all and can take it all. Maybe the message in all the storms isn't about climate. Maybe it's more about taking a stance. God makes his stance pretty easy to follow. Maybe the issue is the U.S. government's failure to recognize biblical law as God's warning.

Ecclesiastes
Chapter 7 Verse 8

The end of a matter is better than its beginning,
and patience is better than pride.

NIV

Chapter 14

Taylorsville

August 2006

THE THANKSGIVING AFTER GRANDMA DIED was a first for Gramps and me. He hadn't missed one Thanksgiving with Grandma since World War II and I hadn't ever missed a Thanksgiving with my kids either. Well, Grandma had died and Jen was taking the kids out of town. It's safe to say the two of us were a little lost that year.

Since the divorce, I was staying more and more with Gramps in his spare bedroom. I'd tell people it was because he needed the help. Which he did. However, being around someone, anyone, especially Gramps, was as good for me as it was for him. I stayed with him for Thanksgiving.

That Thursday morning, I woke up and called the kids, my brothers, and a few friends. It was just a holiday call wishing everyone well and giving them my love. I had those calls placed by nine in the morning. Gramps was already awake, but had no one to call. By 9:01 we were both staring at the TV and an empty refrigerator. To say we poorly planned our first turkey day alone is an understatement.

We talked a little off and on for the next hour, but about nothing with substance or purpose. Just conversations from both of us back and forth trying to ease the boredom. Roughly around 10:30 Gramps hit me with it.

"You ever play any cards?"

"Like card games, or like poker?" I responded.

"Yeah, poker. Like in a casino?"

That's all it took. Just across the river, about 45 minutes away, was a casino with a great card room. At 10:30 that morning, Gramps and I were in t-shirts and our boxers, bored stiff, nothing to do, and not a meal planned for the entire day. We were dressed and on the road. He moved faster than I've seen him move in years. I had never played cards with Gramps and we were both so excited to do something that the drive was a blur.

The casino was a short drive into Indiana. A place with lots of gaming for whatever your interests were. On Thanksgiving Day, the place was packed. Gramps and I talked about eating there on the drive over. I'm guessing we aren't the only ones who didn't have dinner plans.

That Thanksgiving might forever be my favorite of all time. Gramps and I played cards all day and late into the night and we both did well. We hit the buffet not once, but twice. We played right next to one another and when we weren't in the hand, we were goofing around and laughing about anything and everything.

In the truck on the way home, both of us were tired and alone in our thoughts. I was thinking about the prior summer. I didn't have the kids over to see him more than once or twice and I hadn't done a single thing with him all summer. *What a crappy grandson*, I thought. Gramps was probably my best friend and I hadn't played cards with him or taken him to so much as a movie. We hadn't even sunk a single worm in a lake. All that would change over the next couple of years.

Taylorsville is a town in Kentucky as well as Indiana. I've been in Kentucky most of my life and haven't been to either place and haven't heard of either one of them before today. Both towns, one due north of Louisville, and one just southeast of Louisville are so small you could miss them driving by if you blinked. Driving from Gramp's house to one is about an hour. Driving to the other one is about an hour and a half. How could two neighboring states have a town named the same so close to one another?

Taylorsville, Kentucky has a really nice fishing hole, Taylorsville Lake. I heard this morning that the lake has lots of views, good water, and great fishing. The other one in Indiana? Well, I never found a fishing hole, a lake, pond, river, or gutter full of water. And believe me, this morning I tried.

I hadn't been to Gramps' place in a couple days, but out of the blue yesterday he called with nothing else to say, other than that he was going fishing. He called me and said he was going fishing in the morning and asked if I wanted to come. I had the kids Saturday night, but Jen was going to pick them up early Sunday morning for church.

"Heck yeah, Gramps! Jen is picking the kids up about 7:30 on Sunday and I have all day off. Where we going?

"Taylorsville!" He said like a man on a mission. "And I ain't waiting neither. I'd like to be there before sun's up, so if you're coming, I'll meet you there."

"Okay. Where we meeting?" I asked.

"The northern part. See you in the morning," and he hung up the phone.

Well that was my first mistake of the weekend. I've heard of Taylorsville. Never been there or driven by it that I could remember. I couldn't tell you if Taylorsville was in Kentucky, Indiana, or Texas. I didn't ask for a single direction other than where he was going. And all Gramps said was north. Taylorsville, Indiana was roughly 120 some odd miles from my driveway. That sounded like the kind of distance that Gramps would travel.

As he's gotten older, anything more than a two-hour drive really starts to wear him down. My drive was definitely north too, straight up Interstate 65.

The first gas station I pulled up to in Taylorsville had a guy named Brad working the register. I filled up and asked where the live bait was. He explained that they didn't carry any bait and didn't carry any fishing tackle. Further, if I needed a fishing license for Indiana, I'd need to go a little further north toward Edinburgh or turn south and head toward Lowell.

"Well where's the lake?" I asked.

"What lake?" Brad asked

"Taylorsville Lake!" I answered.

"Taylorsville Lake in Kentucky? Brad asked with a slight hint of confusion on his face.

"Kentucky?" I repeated after him.

"Yep. You're looking for Taylorsville Lake a little over two hours south, a little southeast from here. Damn good fishing. Where you from anyway?"

With a sheepishly annoyed and embarrassed look on my face I responded, "Kentucky."

He didn't say another word. He didn't have too. He smirked and I just stood there shaking my head. He could see how pissed off I was with nobody to blame except myself. *Are you kidding me?* I thought. *I'm right about two hours into my morning, and now looking at lunchtime before hitting Taylorsville Lake, Kentucky!* Brad pulled out a map and showed me exactly what I feared. Taylorsville, Kentucky was no more than an hour east from my driveway.

"Once you get there, hit the northern part. That's the best fishing area," Brad included.

Of course, it was, Gramps already new that. He told me the northern part. He was probably worn out reeling in bass. All I'm going to wear out is my butt driving today. I settled up with Brad on gas and turned away to walk out as Brad mentioned one last thing.

141

"Well pal, maybe someone doesn't want you heading that direction."

I stopped and turned back around after the odd comment. "Why would you say that?"

"Because that plane that went down over near Lexington."

"What? I haven't heard. What happened?"

"Don't know much. It wasn't one of those big jets, something similar only carrying 50 people. I don't think any of them survived. Poor folks," he said shaking his head.

I told Brad to have a good day and thanks for the help. I ran off into my truck and found a news channel on the radio covering the crash. At the same time, I started heading south, back toward Kentucky. Five minutes ago, I was going fishing. Now? I wasn't sure if I was going fishing or if I was going to look for "him."

Either way, I was heading south and then would need to go east on Interstate 64. If I turned south off I-64 toward Taylorsville, I figured it was going to take another 20 to 30 minutes. Gramps would probably be annoyed about me being this late. If I kept on I-64 towards the crash site, it would be about 30 to 40 minutes. Gramps might be pissed if I didn't make it all.

Once I hit I-64, I knew I was going. It had been a while since visiting, or rather touring any of the hell holes "he" had left in his wake. The information was sporadic on the radio. For some odd reason, one person survived this morning. One of the pilots, and that's it; 49 others died in what would be called a pilot error.

I had flown in and out of Blue Grass Airport before, so I knew that part of Lexington where the airport was located. Where I was going exactly and what I was going to see once I got there, well, I didn't know. I figured there would be more information on the radio or at minimum, I could see activity around the crash site.

As I passed the exit to Taylorsville Lake, I felt guilty. Gramps was expecting me, and fishing was one thing we both loved. Sometimes loved more than anything or anyone else. I didn't have a way to contact him, but I thought he'd give up waiting soon if he hadn't already. Heck, by the time I was actually in the area, he would have already been fishing for the better part of the day. That assumption was the last mistake of my day.

I drove around Lexington and really couldn't find much. Not much of a place to sight see, that is. I didn't have my camera or binoculars with me. I hadn't planned this trip and was just winging it. It was still early afternoon by the time I arrived.

Years back at the Oklahoma City bombing site, I had a front row view of the building across the street, I was in the middle of the hell in Katrina, and in Waco, Texas I had a vantage point from the hillside. But for this crash site I had nothing.

I drove around looking for someplace where I could stop and check things out. The more I drove around, the less I could seem to find. As with other times before, I was not so sure that coming here was my best idea.

There was a service road that the police and emergency personal seemed to be using. As the day wore on, I thought that my only chance to get a glimpse of "him" was along that road. Possibly coming or going. I made my way to the best intersection I could and camped out in a place where I could go un-noticed and still "check out" every vehicle and every person. After all, in Colorado at that high school, "he" was driving off in a car when we last exchanged glances.

I thought I'd wait until about eight before heading home. That would put me back home around ten. Plus, around 8:30 it was getting dark enough that sightseeing after that point would be a waste. All I was really hoping to get today was lucky. Maybe I could get a glance. If "he" was here, either walking or driving around like before, "he" might be in and out on this service road.

My grandmother warned my brothers and me more than once about 1st Peter 5:8. "Be alert and of sober mind. Your enemy the devil prowls around like a roaring lion looking for someone to devour." To many people, that verse is simple. If you don't watch out for yourself, the devil will. If there are errors in your decisions, the devil will find an easy path into your life.

Grandma always asked what we were up to. When, why, and where we had been, but also where we might be going. She wanted to meet each one of our friends. At times, she drove my brothers and me crazy. I can only imagine how crazy she drove my mother when she was growing up. Sitting here, I can only smile about how much we fought them on everything.

1st Peter 5:8 is a warning. How often might our plans or roads traveled in life lead to destruction? How often do we start the day doing one thing and the world turned inside out because of a poor decision? How often do we partner with someone in business or in love, and it's years before we realize the errors of our mistake? I was right there waiting on the street corner. Could "he" just be in the next car coming my way? *Be alert and of sober mind.*

The day was quickly becoming night. Not a single sight or even likeness of him much less a sense that he's been here. It was looking like another wasted trip. The radio still said that everyone died in the plane crash; 49 people, except the pilot.

I decided around eight in the evening to head back home. A little earlier than I previously planned. The whole darn day was wasted. I planned on fishing with Gramps and ended up looking for "him" at a plane crash site. On the drive home, the more I thought of it, the more upset with myself I became for not going fishing.

I still didn't know what I was going to tell Gramps, but he'd understand. Fishing and poker were just about the only two reasons I could get him out of the house anymore. The entire way home, I felt worse and worse for choosing to search for "him" instead of fishing. I've said this a hundred times, but I'm done looking for "him."

Just after ten at night when I was on Gramps' street I came up on something odd. He was never out late. Never. I don't think in all the years I lived with him while in high school, or the years afterward, I never knew him to be out past sundown. As I approached his house, I knew something was up.

His truck wasn't in the driveway. I sat in my truck with all kinds of thoughts running through my head. I turned off the engine and sat there. The window was down and the silence was almost painful. I could hear dogs barking blocks away. The sound of an airplane 30,000 feet above me was loud. I continued to sit and wonder where in the world he could be. Guilt began to set in. I chose to go to a plane crash site instead of fish with my grandfather. What the hell was I thinking? I had probably 200 thoughts of where he might be. I continued to just sit and wait. Is there a chance he's just late? Maybe he had so much fun that he's just running behind? Maybe he met another friend? But who? At someone's house? Again though... who? I drove just about the same journey home as he would have taken so I doubt his truck has an issue. And then I noticed something.

What the hell is on his front door? From the cab of my truck I could see what looked like a note. I felt relief as he probably left me a note saying that he got home safe and went out some place else. I got out and went to the door. What I thought was relief turned into my worst fear just seconds later.

It was a note written not by my grandfather, but by a Kentucky State Trooper. The note read... "James. Your grandfather has had a medical emergency. He has been transported to a hospital just outside Taylorsville Lake. The staff needs you there immediately."

The note was left at 2:45 p.m. Over seven hours ago.

James
Chapter 1 Verse 26

*Those who consider themselves religious and
yet do not keep a tight rein on their tongues deceive
themselves, and their religion is worthless*

NIV

Chapter 15

Unexpected Surprises

August 2007

BY THE SUMMER OF 2007, I was on my third job in the last couple of years. Again I found myself bouncing around from restaurant to restaurant trying to find something that fit. I became less tolerant of the hours, and for being such a people person, the staff and customers really began to wear on my nerves. The restaurant business had at one time been very good to me. But now it was a struggle to get out of bed and get to work each day.

I had no clue what I could do outside my current experience as a restaurant manager. The only other thing I knew or ever did was that short stint of driving the truck and trailer with Gramps way back when. That sure as hell was off the board. I was desperately looking to do something else.

Ideally, I needed something with weekends off and maybe some free time in the evenings. A nine to five with regular vacations and holiday time off. I could be a better father and I could possibly start dating on a more serious level with a better and more consistent schedule. While thinking about options and dreaming about a career, two events happened that forced the issue.

First, was my new boss. He was hired from an outside restaurant chain and somehow became my direct supervisor immediately. Did I say I was struggling at work? Yeah, possibly my big boss already knew something. Anyway, I hated the guy and I don't hate anyone. There wasn't one thing I liked about the man. I even hated his wife. Why? Probably because she was the ugliest creature ever born and had an unpleasant attitude to match. Even their kids were poorly disciplined and were well on their way to being ugly, rude, annoying adults. I couldn't wait to find a way out and be rid of this man and his family once and for all.

The second thing that summer was Minnesota. For a guy who loves fishing as much as I do, I seem to do it less and less all the time. I was told once that fishing in Minnesota was about as close to heaven as you could get. All I needed that summer was a reason, any reason, and I'd be on my way. Well on August 2nd, I had that reason.

My personal goal to find "him" really hadn't had any traction in a while. I still read papers every morning and spent free time surfing the web hoping to just grab a glimpse or read something about his handy work. I can't go to a store, a mall, or even a gas station without eyeballing every man who even comes close to "his" description.

There has been an endless supply of misery out and about in the world. Still plenty of violence and daily acts of "are you kidding me?" Every day I swear "he" is growing more bold, brave, and evil. I haven't been on a road trip in some time trying to find "him," but the evening of August 1st came and would change that yet again.

While running some errands that evening I heard the I-35 bridge collapsed in Minneapolis. It wasn't a terrorist attack, a barge hadn't run into it from below, there wasn't an earthquake or any other cause from Mother Nature, but something or "someone" had caused that bridge to fall.

The early reports said that several had been killed, many were missing, and the injured would reach well over 100. I was working an evening shift and when I arrived at the restaurant, all the TVs had their regular programming interrupted with the horrible news. Oddly, I was already at battle with my boss that evening over a variety of things. This was all I needed. I called him and told him I would lock up and he could come get the key. I had worked my last shift managing people who hated flipping burgers. I was on my way to Minnesota the next day, some ten hours later.

The drive was roughly 800 miles. I left the following morning with a poor plan to say the least. I knew Minneapolis was in Minnesota, and I knew Minnesota was north. I grabbed my usual road supplies, but this time grabbed some fishing gear. The only thing before last night that I knew for sure was that Minnesota has some of the best fishing. I'd never been, but while heading out again looking for "him," I surely wasn't going to pass up the opportunity.

The drive was quick. Before I knew it, I was in Minneapolis a little before dark. The drive was relaxing, and that part of the country was some of the best I've ever seen. It doesn't have the mountains like Colorado, but the colors reminded me of the same. The mass of trees was incredible to see. As I had heard, the farther north from Kentucky you drive, you can find water just about anywhere. Lakes, rivers, and ponds were everywhere.

As I approached the city, from what I could tell, it looked like a popular place to be. I was shocked at how large it looked from the distance. Minneapolis, I had always thought, was some frozen wasteland with nothing more than a football team. The Vikings had been to four super bowls and were beaten up in each of them. I have this picture of Fran Tarkenton running around on frozen grass. Seems like every picture or video of that man was of him running for his life, and it always looked cold.

I heard that the winters last all year with about three days of summer. I also heard the tallest building might be a grain silo on a farm somewhere on the outskirts of town. I envisioned cattle in the dairy farms out numbering people 100 to one. None of that appeared to be true.

The last hour of the drive before I arrived was spent devising a plan. When I left, I had nothing in mind of where to even start. The local radio stations talked nonstop about where to go and what to do, for locals driving that is. I knew by simply listening that I wasn't going to get anywhere close to that accident site and specifically that bridge. You could only imagine what a mess it was. But I did come up with a decent idea on how to possibly get close. Fishing could be my way in!

If I could park somewhere, grab my pole, cameras, and other supplies, I could hike in along the riverbank. Heck, I could even really do some fishing while checking the crowds for "his" cowardly ass. I had no clue where to park or where to go when approaching the accident site, but I could figure that out in the morning. It was getting dark and I needed to find a resting spot for the night.

As many times before, Walmart was it. Truckers and RV travelers use Walmart for a quick rest at night all the time. I've never once been hassled for sleeping in my truck just a single night. Not to mention any supplies you might need. Walmart was the place. As a bonus, if you are ever got bored, simply walk into Walmart and strike up a conversation with someone. Anyone! You could dig up some information from just about anyone at Walmart. I found one not too far away from the accident site and bunked down in the front seat for the night. Tomorrow would probably be a long day and I would need to start bright and early.

Just as I thought, it was early. A phone call at four in the morning was what woke me up. It was Jennifer. There are a couple of guarantees in life. Phone calls in the middle of the night are either good or really, really bad. She was still listed as one of the emergency contacts for Gramps. I picked up and by the way she said "Jim," I knew something was up.

"Jim, your grandfather was found late last night in bad shape by a neighbor."

Jen and I spoke for a few minutes about what had happened. Apparently, he had another stroke, but this one was pretty bad. He couldn't move or speak. She was called by the first responders who found her number just under mine on the fridge at his place.

She had also contacted my brothers and they were all heading to the hospital. They were all going there as soon as possible. Me though? I was a full day's drive away in Minnesota.

Son of a bitch! After I hung up, I was so mad I couldn't even move. This is exactly how that asshole, satan works. Two strokes now, and I'm not around for either one. The first was when that plane went down and I was off looking for "him" rather than fishing with Gramps. And now? Again, I'm off looking for "him" in Minnesota. "He" absolutely knows I'm right behind "him." I'm closer than "he" likes and "he" keeps using poor Gramps to get me off his tail.

As much as I tried to ignore the obvious, this was yet another wasted trip. Blown money on gas, and another job gone. I never even saw the damn bridge in Minneapolis. Gramps was lying in a bed, and I'm not even close to the same state. I started up my truck, left the Walmart parking lot and headed south at four in the morning.

It was over 1,600 miles in less than 24 hours. A long way to drive just to see a little water. I would have loved to check out the bridge site, but Gramp's needs are more important. Once I was back in Fort Knox, I found the center where Gramps was being cared for, a hospice center. The last place a person might go, just to be comfortable until they die. How morbid. The thought was upsetting.

Gramps might have been comfortable, but I however was in hell. As nice as the place was where he was being cared for, walking in gave me the creeps. The staff were all wonderful. You could tell by the cards and flowers that Jennifer and the kids had been by. Both of my brothers had been in and out as well as a few others. I'm not sure if Gramps knew if anyone was there or not. He lay there breathing, unresponsive to any conversation.

This stroke was much more severe than the other one a few years back. The doctors said the majority of his brain functions had been cut off from air for too long and parts of his brain were forever gone. Actually, other than breathing, I wasn't sure what else he could do. He was struggling greatly.

Teary eyed and feeling as low as I had in some time, I knew this wasn't good. Obviously, I'm not a doctor nor God, but I just knew the end was near. Gramps was the last of my elders. Mom and Dad have been gone for some time, Grandma had died a few years back, and now I was going to be the oldest in our family.

I sat there for a few hours. I talked to Gramps now and then hoping for some kind of reaction, but I got nothing. I chatted briefly with hospital staff coming in and out of the room. Nothing specific, just random pleasantries. They all seemed to genuinely care for my grandfather.

It was late and I needed a quick bite to eat. I hadn't eaten a thing all day. A nurse directed me down the hall to some vending machines. Cheetos, some Twizzlers and a cup of hot chocolate sounded good. I planned on being back in just a few minutes.

When I got to the break room, a guy in front of me was trying to make a selection. He stood in front of one machine repeatedly starting and then abruptly stopping the process. I'm sure my tensions were high, but he was really starting to annoy me. Although it had only been a minute or two, it appeared that he could not figure out how to operate the hot drink dispenser.

I mean it was brutally tough. You had one of three buttons to pick from. Coffee, decaf, or hot chocolate. It was an old styled machine that dropped a paper cup into place and would dispense your beverage of choice after making a selection by touching one of the three buttons. Any monkey could accidentally push a button and bam! Coffee ten seconds later. I was really losing my patience and could feel my temper escalating.

This had been a crappy day all-around. My grandfather was dying down the hall, and all I'd like to do is get a cup of hot chocolate. The joker in front of me either can't read or might actually be trying to piss me off. Maybe he was having a bad day, too. Regardless, the only thing that stopped me from ringing his neck from behind was thinking about what Gramps would do right now. Well? To be honest, Gramps probably would offer to help.

Trying to sound upbeat and friendly, I asked, "Hey fella, can I help you with that selection?"

He sluggishly turned his head and glanced at me briefly. I caught the entire side of his face. I looked at him straight in the eye. He didn't say a word after turning his head. The silence seamed forever. He didn't have to utter a word. The minute we made eye contact, I knew exactly who he was and once he started talking, it only confirmed it.

"Well Jim, that would be great. I can't read a word on this machine," he responded.

I have been asked the same question no less than a hundred times for several years: what was I going to do once I found "him?" My brothers, Jen, my children, my grandparents, and every other family member or friend have all asked me the same question. If I was ever to find him, what was I going to do?

Well, here he was. Satan himself. The evil one. The devil in human disguise. I've been all over the country looking for this man or thing and here he is. I'd seen him before not just once, but twice in person. They say the third time's a charm. This was no doubt the same man standing right before me. I stood completely frozen. To be honest, I have never been able to really answer that question. Year after year, person after person. I'd tell them my story and I always received the same question. What would I do if I ever found him?

To be honest, I've always sort of envisioned killing him. Where I'd be and how I'd do it. It's probably a bad thing to admit, but it's the truth. Payback, perhaps, for what he did not only to my parents, but to so many other innocent people. Probably no less than a thousand times I've thought about harming "him" in some fashion. Maybe I could use a weapon of some sort. A gun might not do it. After all, "he" is supernatural, and a bullet probably would be futile. Maybe a sword or knife through his heart? Like killing a vampire? I'm not sure; that seems childish. Maybe if I just choke him out, grab his neck and squeeze with every muscle I ever had. I would take his life just like he's done each and every time to his victims since the beginning of time.

I've also thought year in and year out that just an earful from me might be effective. I mean after all, who else tells this guy off? I might, just to put this creature in his place. A verbal assault, not as violent, but if done correctly, could be just as effective. He is a weak creature and I know he can be broken. It might sound corny, but I want to tell him what I think about all of his BS. Maybe I would just ask him what his problem is. What are you hoping to achieve? Ask him if he understands or knows the amount of rage and hate the world has against him. I could ask him if he understands how billions upon billions of people around the planet think he's an a-hole. Maybe I could shame him into hiding. At minimum, God might be proud of me for telling this "thing" off.

It was only a brief second or two since he replied to my question and before I could say or do anything, before I could respond, he'd continue with a smirk and a small laugh, "Jim, finally we get to meet you."

With that same odd grin on his face that I've grown to hate, he extended his hand like anyone would do when they say hello. I'm not sure what shocked me more. His gesture of friendliness? Or the fact that I actually shook his hand.

Still frozen and now puzzled by the random meeting, all I

could say was, "What do you mean great to meet me? And who is 'we?'"

He looked over behind me and nodded over toward the waiting room opposite the vending area where we were standing. "Yes, *we* are pleased to meet you. Both Jesus and I."

I looked in the direction he had pointed--toward the waiting room and then back quickly again. I wasn't looking for anyone else. I had been looking for this "guy," or "thing," for too long to remember. Before I could continue, I confusedly muttered, "Did you say Jesus?"

Matthew
Chapter 27 Verse 21-22

Which of the two do you want me to release to you?
asked the Governor. "Barabbas" they answered.
"What shall I do then, with Jesus who is called Christ?"
asked Pilate. "Crucify him!

NIV

Chapter 16

Pontius Pilate

PONTIUS PILATE WAS THE SIXTH ROMAN PROCURATOR (Governor), of Judea from about 26 to 36 A.D. His administrative center was at Caesarea. His governorship was contemporary with the ministry of John the Baptist, and then of Jesus Christ.

Pilate was not a friend to the Jews. "Mutual contempt" could sum up that relationship. He apparently avoided visits to Jerusalem as much as possible. Pilate was a highly political man, and the Jews seemed to know that their threatened complaints to Pilate's superiors in Rome could get the governor to act in their favor. The release of a convicted murderer in place of Jesus Christ, an innocent man, is a perfect example.

For whatever it may be worth, Pilate did try many times to have Jesus released because he knew Jesus was completely innocent of any crime. Pilate's wife also tried to get Jesus released. She had once sent Pilate a note by messenger, "Don't have anything to do with that innocent man, for I have suffered a great deal today in a dream because of Him." (Matthew 27:19). Scholars years later would say Pilate's wife may well have been among the first generation of Christians.

It was Pilate who had the sign placed over the cross. That was the Roman custom, normally used to publicly declare the crime for which the person was crucified. In Jesus' case, Pilate had the sign say, "This is Jesus, The King of the Jews." (Matthew 27:37) Which was no crime at all, as Pilate was fully aware. It was merely a sarcastic comment aimed at the religious authorities who had Jesus unjustly condemned to death for their own political reasons.

After learning that Jesus had died, Pilate released His Body to Joseph of Arimathea to be buried in the tomb.

***

I HAD PREPARED FOR THIS DAY longer than I can remember. Anticipating this event had occupied my thoughts longer than most other memories I can recall. I know exactly how I felt when I first realized who "he" was. Since the day I recognized his existence, I have always wanted a piece of his ass. I've never thought of harming anyone before in my life. But with this guy, it would be fair to say I had it in the back of my mind more than a handful of times that I wanted to kill him or at least do some grand bodily harm.

I've been asked a hundred times, "Jim, what are you planning if you ever do find him? Jim, what are you going to say to the thing? Jim... satan, the devil? You're going to track down and do something to the devil?"

Yeah, yeah, yeah. I don't care what anyone has said. I've lost jobs, my wife, and few friends along the way. The amount of money wasted? All of it, I don't care. This was something I had to do. It came to my mind one day and has lived in my heart ever since. If needed, I was going to spend the rest of my life finding this...this beast. And now, just like everyone predicted, I've got no clue what to say or do.

"Pilate?" I asked. You said your name is Pilate? Is that what you call yourself?" I asked in a temper.

"Well yes, that is my name," he calmly replied.

Before I had a chance to ask anything else or even respond, he would add. "Yes, my name is Pontius Pilate."

"Are you not also known as satan? Or the devil, or the evil one?" I asked.

The man or creature before me stood with a shocked looked on his face. Frozen for just a brief moment. This is the same face I'd seen before. Actually, not just his face: but his build, hair, facial expressions...it was all the same. This guy was the same man I've seen face to face back in the hills and in those pictures on my grandfather's couch. The same goofy grin, the same long forehead, and that same odd accent in his voice. No doubt about it, this was the guy.

"Jim, although this isn't how things are usually done, it is still a great day to meet you again. I'm guessing you would like an understanding of events? Why I have now come before you again?" he asked me.

This man or thing in front of me whom calls himself Pilate, extended his hand as a friendly gesture and smiled at me. Exactly the same way he did on the dirt road back when I was a teenager the day my parents died. I had never heard his voice before that day and the minute I heard it again, I felt a kind of resting peace. Not because of him, but maybe it brought me closer to a memory of my parents. An odd peace as a few minutes ago I was a little unnerved at finally meeting the guy I thought I believe to be satan. Even more odd...I actually shook his hand.

"I guess we'll discuss the satan deal in a minute, but on a different note, I've always believed and known Pilate as a bad man. He or you, or whatever you are is the guy who killed Jesus, and now you're telling me that that guy in the corner is Jesus and you're Pilate? I'm just not sure I understand," I asked while shaking his hand.

I have lived my entire adult life with this idea of tracking down satan. Never much a plan for what I was going to say or do, but still my plan was to track "him" down. I've succeeded, but now this? There's no way I could tell anyone about this. Pilate and Jesus in the same room with *me* of all people. Oh, this will be good. What few friends and family I have left would be running out the door when they hear this one.

I continued, "I gotta tell ya, I haven't quite worked out how you haven't aged in 20-plus years, but I'm not falling for this one bit. The devil is best known as a deceiver. The greatest liar of them all."

"Well, Jim, that would be true. If I was the devil, deceiving would be one of my greatest talents. Perhaps I could comment on my age first?"

"Sweet, I'd love to hear this one," I replied with skepticism.

It hasn't been about 20 years as you have suggested. Rather I have yet to age a single day in almost 2,000 years. I know you and I met just a few years past, and do I not look the same today as I did back then? Your grandfather and I met over half a century ago. Although it was just briefly, I was the same man in appearance that I am now. Hard to understand, I assume?"

"Hard to understand? Are you kidding me? That's impossible!" I said. "It's a lie. You can't say one more thing to me to prove differently. I'm a pretty simple man with nothing more than a little college education, but there's no way. Humans are born, we live, we age, and then we die!"

"Well, let's start with a question perhaps," Pilate suggested, "and if I may, would you allow me to ask the first question to you?"

Feeling a little stunned by the entire event unfolding I said with sarcasm, "Sure, sounds great. I can't wait."

Pilate then asked, "What is it that you know of me? Please, tell me all. Maybe from your lessons of history? Or maybe from the readings from your Bible? Tell me, from your understanding, who am I and what have I done in the history of man?"

"Well, Pilate was the guy who killed Jesus," I began.

Pilate quickly jumped back into my response with a clarification request to my answer. "Weren't the many hours in the sun and the outdoors having just been through a crucifiction the reason for Jesus' final breath?"

"Okay, fine. After you tortured Jesus, he was nailed to a cross and left to die!" I hastily rebut, almost annoyed.

"Is that it? Is that all you know of me?"

"Well, I did read that you, I mean Pilate, had a wife at the time who warned him not to touch Jesus. Something about a dream she had about bad things."

"Yes, my wife Proculla. A beautiful woman. Also known to many as Saint Proculla or Saint Claudia. All the names are of the same person. Proculla Claudia Pilate was my wife. Is that the extent of your knowledge of me? I would have hoped that you had read that I tried to defend Jesus. It was I who questioned the governor's authority whether or not to torture and crucify him. I believe that it has been written in the history books and your Bible that it was I, Pilate, who told many that Jesus had committed no sin. Did you not know of these things?"

"Well, now that you say that, it all sounds familiar. But tell me, if you are Pilate then why do you keep showing up in my life? This is several times now, and even before me, you were in my grandfather's life. Is that also true? Why do you keep showing up at these horrible events of death and destruction?" I paused. "Wait, before you even go there, you say you are traveling with Jesus? Jesus Christ.... the Son of God?"

The man before me, claiming to be Pilate, leaned back against the wall. Kinda relaxing, almost making himself comfortable for a chat. I was busy with a steady line of questions. Needing, or rather asking for proof maybe faster than he could even respond. He never took his eyes off me and with a shake of his head, puckered his lips and sighed.

"As I said earlier, this is not the usual way of doing things for us. I find it hard myself to understand today's meeting.

Nobody has ever tracked us down and discovered who we are. Certainly, if they had, I would not have thought anyone might accuse me of being the devil. Why would you think I'm the devil?" he questioned.

The man who claimed to be Pilate stood shaking his head slightly. I thought about harming this man--at the least, giving him a piece of my mind. But I find myself drawn to his presence. The way he speaks, his pecular voice, and oddly enough, he, is inviting.

Before I could answer his question, he softly blurted out, "Odd."

"Odd what?" I replied.

"Odd that I tell you I'm Pilate, I tell you that the man I travel with sitting in the room behind you is our brother Jesus Christ, son of our Holy Father and the first thing we discuss is my age." Somewhat laughing under his breath, he again said, "Odd."

"Well Jim, perhaps if I just spoke for a few moments. Maybe in my introduction and explanation you could possibly have some questions answered. I do understand why you might have so many. I also understand that if you presume me to be another person that might also add emotion. So be it. Not long after you and I first met in the mountains following the passing of your parents, my friend Jesus told me that in a short time, I would see you again. This would normally mean that your own passing was within a short time..."

"Wait a minute, did you say friend? Your friend Jesus would tell you?" I asked clearly with both skepticism and disbelief.

"Yes, my best friend. Now shall I continue?"

As the man before me, so called Pilate, continued his story, I haven't lost my belief that he was the devil. This was him alright. satan. This is how it works, I guess. Most people never run in direct contact with him. My family and I just so happened to have seen him a few times. At some point, I'll find an opening in his story and call BS. Something won't add up. This was the start of another great lie. Many, many years ago the same story was told a little differently by a snake into the ear of Eve.

"To my surprise, I was not coming for your passing or even to prevent it. But over the years, recent ones at that, all over the country I'd look up and there you were. It's almost become a question of a friendly nature between Jesus and me. I think a joke as you might call it. I'd ask Jesus, 'You think Junior will be here today? Long before we would ever leave in the morning.'"

"Junior?" I asked.

"Yes, Junior. I believe it was your earthly father who called you that. Correct?" Pilate would question.

Completely shocked, I responded, "Ahh...Yes, he did."

The last person to call me Junior was my father. I haven't heard that name since he died. Not one person, friend, or family member has ever called me Junior since that day. It was my dad's nickname for me. I am sure the man standing before me, Pilate or not, is the devil. However, or whoever he was, he had my full attention.

Pilate continued, "Do you remember making eye contact at the school in Colorado? I was in shock. I knew the minute you looked at me you were different. For some reason, here's this man from a place called Kentucky following us. I will tell you the truth, I didn't know what to say or do. I ran off like a scared animal, straight in the back of our vehicle. It wasn't until I questioned Jesus and asked him specifically about you that he told me. Jesus has known from day one. However, I had to be told. Jesus told me that Junior is one of the special ones. Someone we could let run a little. Perhaps figure things out on his own, even if it might be the hard way. Doing unholy kinds of things. No matter where you were or what you were doing, you'd find your place back to the eyes and heart of Jesus."

"Why did you call me Junior? Only one person has ever called me Junior," I asked.

"Well, your earthly father did. When I was asked by your

father to watch over you and your brothers, he told me that I could depend on you. He told me Junior is a good, young man that we could lean on. One whom we could seek help from. One way or another, Jr. would always do the right thing. As a matter of fact, the last thing your dad ever said to me was that it may not be for years to come, but his boy Jim, or Junior as he called you, would be his little preacher."

At this point, I stared at him with my mouth open and completely in shock. I'm not really sure what to think. I guess it wasn't tough to believe that the devil knew about me as well. I heard once in Sunday School that good and evil have had a history long battle for the souls of every man, woman, and child. This is the way things are done. Satan too would know things about me.

"But yes, to answer your question, I was the man ultimately responsible for the death of Jesus Christ. I had what you would call a job. I was a Roman Politician. However, I worked outside the arena of politicians. Back then, we all did. Imagine if you will, being a governor who had the responsibilities of the police. Although we did squabble at times, sometimes endlessly, we had responsibilities outside of our office. When Jesus of Nazareth became known to me and others back then, it was my job, rather, I had to deal with that."

"Deal with it? What do you mean?" I asked.

"I'll ask you in this manner: who do you know that gets a lot of attention, good or bad? Maybe even both. An actor, an athlete, or an official in today's government. Some leader in business, a school principle, or a clergyman. Pick someone you may know, or have come to know. Now, when you have that person come to mind, think of this. That person, either good or bad, make them in your head 1,000 more than what they are. Do you understand this task?"

"Yes, I think so. And yes, I know of a person. I'm thinking of them right now," I answered.

"Good. Now imagine, if you will, this person whom you know to be good or bad, for this purpose it makes no difference, I need not know. Now if I told you every person whom you would come into contact with also knew of this person, some may think good, some may think badly. Would this be possible?"

"Absolutely," I respond.

"You are thinking of Jesus, are you not?"

"Well yeah, how did you know?" I asked.

"Every child of God, from every corner of the earth knows of that man." He pointed toward the other room where I could see him sitting.

"Imagine a world where Jesus was not a man's name just written in the books of time. Imagine a time where miracles or teachings were not just read about, but witnessed. Finally, image a time and place where a man who would challenge the law of many for the better of the few, even if that meant death by crucifixion. Yes, Jim, I had to deal with it! I had to deal with that man named Jesus Christ. I came to know Jesus through whispers in my ear. Whispers from those who I served, whispers from those who served me. I believed them all. He was not a Godly man. He was Liar. He was not born as a deliverer. This man was born of un-holy relations, a relationship that was against the law. He was a threat for all the good in the world. Our plans were not his. His stories, his work, his teachings all would blind any man who would listen. He robbed them all of life. You could say I put that man on the cross because I, too, wanted to protect our lives. We needed to rid ourselves of the evil one."

"And?" I asked.

We both stood there looking into each other's eyes. To tell you the truth, I had no clue what to ask. I wasn't sure what to think, much less say. I knew this story. At a minimum, you heard it in some form or another at Easter and Christmas. Add another half dozen stories and references to his death through the average year and I'd guess 10-12 times each year of my life I've heard the story that this man stood before me telling. It was scary though. I'd never heard the words used that I'm hearing now. Even the way he spoke. I'd never been told in detail and with such a matter of fact style as I was told just then. The way the story was told, one might think that man before me was actually there.

"And? And what?" Pilate would ask me back.

"Well what did you do next? You crucified him and then had him buried in the tomb. Is that correct?"

"Yes, but I'm in awe that you didn't know that," Pilate would ask almost like he was prying for me to continue.

"Yeah, but you are here now, you say that you are traveling with Jesus who sits in the room behind us. I guess I would like to hear how you are standing before me today?"

"Yes, it might be the correct time to answer that," he said with a grin.

"Jim, I truly hope you understand, this event today is a first for me. I have never told this story to anyone. I have never had to. I am not the teacher that Jesus is. I speak as well as I can. But at some point, you'll understand and come to believe me when I tell you my name is Pilate. I was born in the spring almost 2,100 years ago. I was a good student and a grand athlete. We played games of a different nature back when I was young. I was a good young man. I got into politics shortly before marring my wife. I enjoyed the power of government. People would look up to me and listened to what I said. If they did not listen, well, remember what I told you? I was also the police." We both giggled.

"I was the man responsible for the arrest and death of Jesus Christ. The day before his crucifixion was a bad day. Although I wouldn't admit that at the time. I knew of the thousands of believers Jesus had. Many were old friends, even family. Even my wife. My best friend, whom I trusted with secrets known to no one, would tell me of a dream of pain and suffering for me if I hurt the Son of God. I knew I was doing wrong. Jesus' crime was being honest. Jesus' crime was telling people of a better way.

Jesus would speak of love and ask that you respect and believe in only one God. The people loved Jesus. The more they loved him, the more our government and our leaders hated him. But it wasn't the day before his crucifixion that was tough. That day was bad, but the days following would be days that I have never forgotten."

Completely drawn into this story, I said, "Some bad times?"

"At the time, the worst. The worst I've ever known. I had a hand in killing Jesus Christ. Try explaining that one to your friends and family."

"Oh, I hear you. Try telling your friends and family about an endless search to find the devil." We both exchanged smiles.

Pilate continued telling me of the days after the crucifixion. He went on with stories and tales that I couldn't believe. Although some sounded familiar, most of them I had never heard before. They were hard to hear and even harder to believe. Pilate, leaning against the wall in the snack room would continue speaking without interruption. The more he spoke, the more I was drawn in. I stood there listening in disbelief. A half an hour ago, I believed his story was a lie, in fact I was certain of it. But now, I'm not so sure. The words coming from his mouth were more believable than anything I have ever heard. With additional detail, I was more and more unsure exactly whom stood before me.

"I was the first one who would see him. The others didn't want to, but we all knew the truth. But for me, I had to see him to believe it."

"See who?" I asked. I could hardly wait for the response.

Pilate turned his head and again grinned at me and said, "Jesus Christ. That's who."

He continued, "As word spread that Jesus had risen from the dead, I wanted to see him. Everyone did. Word of his resurrection spread across the world like nothing I had ever witnessed before. In mere days, every soul from the edge of every shore knew, and all wanted to witness. Today you have phones and computers to communicate with one another. In my day, we had horses and most of the horses were ridden by people who could not read or write. How that news spread so fast and so far, still amazes me."

Pilate paused, almost in deep reflection or recall of his story, "For me, of course I had a different investment. For three days, I had lived in the hell of knowing all along what we had done was wrong. As I told you, those were bad days. I had no peace. Although I wasn't alone in the decision, it would ultimately fall upon my hands. However, as bad as things were for me the days following the crucifixion, the minute I heard of His resurrection there was a peace in me that I have never lost. I was so hoping, rather praying, for his well-being. I wasn't sure how and to tell you the truth I didn't care how it happened. I just wanted him alive."

"How did you see him?" It was rude of me to interrupt, but it just came out.

"Well, I'll tell you this. You may have read about his followers. Or maybe you have heard stories about those who followed him?"

Again, I would interrupt, "I do know a lot about his disciples. I did go to Sunday School and church often," I threw in, as if I wanted some kind of approval.

"Oh, no. I mean his followers. There were more followers in numbers than than stars in the sky. Not just the twelve. I had little knowledge of how many people not only knew of him, but believed in him. All the more a reminder of what I had done and how wrong I was to have participated. Nevertheless, I did need to see him alive. He was surrounded every hour of the day. I had to remain at a distance. The fear of being killed or crucified myself by someone amongst the mob wasn't what concerned me. The fear of seeing Jesus and answering for my sins, and the fear of being judged face to face was a terrifying thought. I would try to catch sight of him from a distance and I spent the better part of several days trying to get close without being noticed. I slept not, I ate not, and I continued until I witnessed the miracle myself."

168

Paralyzed from shock, I couldn't wait to hear this. "How did it happen? Where were you? When did you see him?" I asked.

"For days, I could not get close enough to catch a glimpse for myself. I could not find the mob with him in the center. As much as I wanted to see him alive, I finally gave up. After a few days of waiting, I decided to leave. Then one evening on my way home, there he was."

"Where?" I asked. Almost barking out at him.

"At my front door. Standing inside the threshold and speaking with my wife Proculla."

"What?" I said, "I had never read that in the bible."

"Yes, the Son of Our Lord God, Jesus of Nazareth, stood at my door waiting to speak with me. I had no doubt that the man standing face to face with me was him. He was the exact man I had ordered to be put to death. He was the same man who was laid into a tomb to rest. Almost a week removed from his crucifixion. Now I became a witness."

Our conversation continued for several minutes. He told me all about what was said between him and Jesus. He also said several things he and Jesus spoke of that day would forever remain private. I guess that makes sense. One of our greatest gifts is the intimacy between God and us all. Special to all of us, but in our own unique way. As I stood there listening to his story, I'll admit, I was confused about what I was hearing, and I had more questions. I listened to Pilate, knowing that I thought he was satan less than an hour ago. Now, I was really unsure. As he continued, another voice came echoing in from the other room.

"Are you two all right over there?"

"Who's that?" I asked Pilate.

Again, with the same smile and cookie eating grin, Pilate would answer, "That's him, that's Jesus Christ. We should probably go say hello."

"Yeah, okay..." I said as my hands started to sweat and my voice cracked.

"But I have one last question for you, maybe two if that's okay?" I asked this question both wanting the answer and all the while wanting to delay meeting Jesus myself. If Jesus was sitting in the room across the hall what on earth would I say to him, and what on earth was he doing here waiting to talk with me?

"Pilate, maybe you can explain later how you're still alive 2,000 years later, but for now I'd rather know why you're traveling with Jesus? Is that possible to ask or even have answered?"

"Possibly. Well, quickly I'll tell you one thing and then we'll go meet Jesus together."

"Okay, that sounds good," I said shaking my head yes.

"The best lesson I could ever teach you was the lesson Jesus taught me at my doorstep. Nothing is more powerful than a man who forgives. Forgive a man of his sin, forget any debts to him, reach your hand to a man in need of comfort or help, and all the while, want nothing in return. Jesus Christ stood at my door and said he was going on a journey. A journey that would take him to every shore and every mountain on earth. He told me his plan was to touch every soul on earth and to meet the children of God, his brothers and sisters, for years to come. He had a plan but was now at my door in need of one thing before he left."

"What, Pilate? What did he need from you?" I couldn't wait for his response.

"He told me he needed a witness. He needed someone who was a believer. He needed someone who could love and be loved. He needed someone who would follow, but at times also lead. He told me these desires and then he asked me something I still can't believe."

"Please, what is it?" I pleaded him to go forward.

"He said he needed a friend and wanted to know if I would accompany him on his journey."

He put his hand on my shoulder almost like a coach escorting a player onto the court and we began walking toward the waiting room.

Jeremiah
Chapter 17 Verse 9

The heart is deceitful above all things and beyond cure.
Who can understand it?

NIV

Chapter 17

SOM

"GEEZ, I THOUGHT MAYBE YOU TWO were having a cocktail or something. Would you like a private table for two with a candle?" He said while shaking his head with a humorous smile. He was being funny and poking at us both for taking so long to join him.

Sarcastically Pilate said, "Well you were correct SOM, he didn't believe me. And truthfully, I still doubt that he does." He looked directly at me almost like he was asking me a question.

Sitting in a chair before me was just an average looking guy. I sat in the chair directly across from him. Average was my first thought about the man. He looked about my age, maybe a few years younger and he looked simple. I have always thought that one day I would meet Jesus. We all do, I guess. I have envisioned the pearly gates and there he would be waiting, waiting to say hello or to help me with the process of getting into Heaven. There would be a bright light glowing from his body or something that felt divine. Maybe even the two of us floating off together. He had long, flowing, kinda curly brown hair, blue eyes, and all he does is smile.

In reality, he was a good-looking man, that's for sure. He had a good head of hair, an unshaven face, and yeah...blue eyes. I'd guess he was close to six feet tall. His face looked relaxed and painless. He had a grin like he's been up to something. When I first walked toward him, I found myself drawn in. His kind face made me want to talk. It was very relaxing. Pilate said this guy was Jesus and even if he wasn't, his demeanor was oddly inviting.

"So, Jim, you're a little shocked I imagine?" He asked with a smile and a little chuckle.

"Shocked? I couldn't tell you how I feel. To be honest, I wasn't even sure what to think."

"I understand. We've had others over the years who didn't believe either. Believe at first, that is."

After about a three second pause, he also included, "But they did believe, all of them, sooner or later!"

"So, you are telling me that you are Jesus Christ?" I asked.

Before he could even answer, I looked in Pilate's direction and asked him, "What did you call him? SOM?"

Pilate shaking his head with a confident voice, "Yes, SOM. That is correct. I think you refer to it as a nickname? SOM is a short name for Son of Man!"

"Ahhh, I guess that makes sense," I said.

Just sitting there, even for that brief time I had nothing to say. I'd prepared for years to meet satan, and now I'm sitting with these two jokers claiming to be Pilate and Jesus Christ and I couldn't find anything, not a single word, to say. I had often thought about how to handle a meeting with satan. What I might say or do, but now this? Every part of Pilate's story just minutes earlier sounded too unreal to really give it a second thought. And now I'm sitting before Jesus Christ?

We probably stood there for ten seconds before anyone said anything. It might have been the longest ten seconds of my entire life. Jesus finally broke the ice.

"Are you still upset with me?" Jesus asked.

"Upset with you?" I was confused by the question so I asked it again. Yes, was how I wanted to answer, as I was at one time very hurt and "upset" with Jesus. But that was years ago after my parents had died.

"Why, yes. My relationship with my father, our God, is a special one. Not that much different than the relationship you had with your father. I'm sure you'll agree that neither of your younger brothers were any less loved, but I know that you had a unique relationship with your father. Am I correct?"

"Ah, yeah. Without a doubt he was my dad, my best friend, my teacher, my protector. He was everything to me," I said.

"So again I ask, are you still upset with me?"

"I'm not sure I follow. What do you mean by upset with you?" For some reason, I wanted to hear a little more explanation about the question from him.

"Are you not James David Thompson? Born the 23rd day of November in the year of 1970?"

"Yes, that's me. How did you know that? Actually...never mind," I said, while nervously laughing and shaking my head because I had just asked a dumb question.

"Several years have passed, but for quite some time you didn't have many kind words about me or about our father after the death of your parents. I know you specifically questioned our intentions and even blamed me for some events in your life. You blamed me for the loss of your parents. Am I correct?"

I stood there frozen. Almost like being busted in a bold-faced lie. My face was turning red and I could feel my heart pounding up through my neck. I'm not sure if I'm more amazed about the fact that I might be actually speaking with Jesus Christ himself, or the fact that this nut case in front of me just jumps out and starts questioning my faith dating back to my parents' death. There was the oddness that if this guy wasn't Jesus, how the hell would he know what he's saying? What he was speaking was 100% truth. I've been upset and angry for years.

"Yeah, I guess for a time there I was upset and questioning why it had happened seemed less painful," I replied. "Maybe I

174

thought by blaming you, or maybe more specifically by blaming God, some of the hurt would go away."

"How's that working out for you?" Pilate interrupted.

"Well I'm not really sure. I did blame God for taking my parents."

"I know, that one night while you were in your last year of school. That spring night when you had the run-in with the police. Remember that?"

Amazed and humored I shook my head yes while giggling.

"Yeah, I believe you gave me a good cursing that night. But take them from you? You didn't own them," Jesus replied.

"Of course I didn't own them, but you know what I mean. Why did you let them die?"

"Well now Jim, you probably know I didn't let them die. Or at least I hope you know that. They died as the result of an accident. My job was to meet them and to say hello," Jesus said with a smile.

"Hello? They both died in a fireball and you were there to say hello?"

"Well sure, what else would you think I would be doing with them?"

Almost annoyed, I continued with the questions. "Okay fine, you wanted to say hello, couldn't you have stopped the accident? They could still be alive today. Why did they have to die that way?"

"Stopping the accident in the mountains would have been tough. And yes, I imagine seeing your parents die the way they did must have been hard to witness. Would it have been better if they had heart attacks or have died suffering from a disease? Or if they had been killed by a weapon from the hand of another man? Maybe if they had died from a lightning strike, from drowning, or even killed in a car accident. Which one of those would have been the best way to die?"

As much as I wanted to argue with him, he was correct. Dying is dying. We will all face it. Death comes to us all. Some early in life, others very late and the rest of us? You just never know.

With a heavy heart I replied, "I guess you are right, it really doesn't matter how, but I've always struggled with how they died. How much pain and suffering they went through. Although it seemed quick, dying that way just seems kind of hard, unnecessary, and unfair."

"Well Jim, what if I told you they didn't suffer at all. Not a single second, as you may think?"

"Really? How could that be possible? I witnessed something that has scarred me forever. Not a single day goes by that I can get that picture out of my head. Every time I even think of the pain and suffering they went through, I've wanted to kick someone's ass."

"Like satan's?" Jesus asked with an odd look on his face.

"Yeah...I guess," I said with a grin. "I've been chasing him for years...umm, I mean *him*, I guess," I pointed to Pilate.

"Well, James, that's foolish. You really think chasing down satan would happen?" Jesus asked. "What might be more foolish is the idea that you think your parents died in pain and suffering."

Jesus looked directly at me. Pilate was the only one who moved as he leaned back in his seat with a look of disgust. Both of them staring at me like we were all in a blinking contest. A contest that I was no doubt going to lose.

"I guess I'm not sure how it works. How could their accident in the mountains have not been painful for them? I know I've always questioned and yes, even blamed you and God, but I'm not sure how to deal with what happened."

"Well James, I know you have read scripture? I believe you have a King James Version of a book that tells of my story?" He questioned. Even though he obviously knew the answer, for some reason he still asked.

"Yeah, sure... but which story?" I asked confused.

I'm not sure if he was annoyed or if he was just asking a question, but Pilate barked out, "The story of Jesus Christ. The Son of Man. Perhaps you have heard of him?"

"Easy, Pilate," Jesus directed his comment as Pilate bit his bottom lip and shook his head like he needed a half second to relax.

I continued almost immediately, "Yeah, I know lots. Not everything, but I do know of Jesus, or you I guess, through my Bible and church, too," I felt like I needed to include that.

Pilate was much more involved, almost in a defensive manner. He folowed up his own question. "What do you know about the story of Jesus Christ?"

We sat there for the next few hours. I'm not quite sure how long, but the sun had long set. I never felt hungry or had a desire to walk around or even to go to the bathroom. We sat and talked for hours about what Jesus Christ, the man sitting before me, came here to do.

For the most part, I sat there and listened in amazement. Pilate and Jesus went back and forth with stories. Along the way, I asked questions or voiced opinions about my beliefs. I was asked questions about my own life in relation to their experiences: what I would have done, where I might have gone, what am I going to do now?

During that time there were some tears, but mostly there were lots of laughs. These two might be the best story telling duo ever. I can't even begin to retell most of those stories. Each of them was believable, but at the same time too hard to comprehend. The stories in the Bible were all validated to me now, told from the people who lived through it. I've always known a lot about Jesus, but I didn't know much of Pilate before that day.

Pilate was not the evil man who had Jesus crucified. He was actually kind, smart, and quite funny. He spoke with authority and was very direct. There was a little edge to his personality. The kind of edge that I assumed you didn't want to cross. Almost like he was the muscle in the relationship.

Story after story, there were two things I started to sense without doubt. The man before me who claimed to be Jesus was doing exactly what I've always heard he does. He tells stories. Lots and lots of stories. I sat there for a couple hours and things that I didn't know how to understand seemed a little easier. One topic that he revisited throughout our conversation was about death and how the faithful know no pain. He was very clear on that.

Both men had a strong accent. Occasionally they caught one another speaking in another language. Only a word or two, but they always looked at me and smile and apologize for speaking it. I'm not sure what the language was, but I can tell you this. Neither one of them was from Kentucky, that's a fact.

In the middle of one story I caught Pilate saying something in that language again. I speak only English, but have worked with all kinds of friends who speak all kinds of languages and this one I couldn't guess where it was from. So, what the heck, I interrupted them and asked the question.

"What language are you speaking?"

Pilate immediately stopped and asked, "Any guesses?"

Every question and statement tonight all seemed like a never-ending test. "Well, I'm not sure," I responded.

"Perhaps a language from a European country? Or even South Africa, maybe Australia?" I was just throwing out anything that might stick. Hoping to get lucky and show them how smart I was.

Pilate shook his head up and down while running his fingers across his mouth, almost like trying to wipe a smile away. Then all he said was, "I've told you before."

"You have?" I questioned.

With a grin on his face he looked at me dead in the eyes and said. "I have. Remember back in the mountains? When your parents left to join our father in Heaven? Your younger brother asked where I was from and I told the three of you then."

I knew what was coming next before he even said it. Goose bumps covered every inch of my arms and the hair shot up on my neck. I thought I was going to throw up. It was the same comment my grandfather had heard back on that boat in World War II.

"I'm not from Europe or Australia, but somewhere in the middle."

Psalms
Chapter 32 Verse 8

I will instruct you and teach you in the way you should go;
I will counsel you with my eye upon you.

NIV

Chapter 18

Enthous. Inspired by God!

WHAT WAS ONCE AFTERNOON quickly became night and before I knew it, the clock on the wall read 8:08 in the evening. Jesus, Pilate, and I sat together for well over six hours talking about all kinds of things.

The area by the lobby where we were sitting had all kinds of activity. Doctors were coming and going, and nurses were running around guiding the constant traffic of family coming in to see loved ones. I thought it was strange that not one single person interrupted us. Almost like we weren't even there.

"So tell me, how long have you guys known about my little deal to find satan, or I guess to find you, Pilate?" I asked.

"Actually, it wasn't until the spring in 1999. Do you remember that day?" Jesus asked.

"Spring of 1999? Wasn't that, Columbine?"

"Yes, the school in Colorado," replied Jesus.

With a serious voice, shaking his head slightly from side to side and with a strained look on his face, Pilate added, "You scared the breath out of me that day!"

Shocked I replied, "I did?"

"Jim, I've seen a lot. I have been all over the earth and what we had to deal with at the school was as hard as it gets. When we got to the car, and I happened to notice you watching me, before I could even ask SOM about it, you were off and running. At me!" We all chuckled a little.

"Hey Pilate, you told me that SOM came from Son of Man, but why that? Why a nick name?" I asked.

"Many years ago, walking around calling him Jesus didn't always go over well. Often, it was almost a distraction with our work. Not many have asked about the nickname SOM, most just consider it a name."

"Ahh... I see. I have another question if that's alright. What do you mean by 'our work?' You have said that a few times now. What exactly are you two doing here?"

It was perfect. I finally had a way to ask. Up until then, we had just been talking about history and how it intertwined in my life and the lives of others. From the very second, I sat down with them, I'd been waiting for the opportunity to ask questions. What are you two doing here? How is this possible? And the biggest question of all, why am I here with you?

There was a lengthy pause after I asked it. Both looked at me, then towards one another and spoke about two maybe three sentences each in that strange language again. At other times during our conversations earlier the language was spoken unintentionally. This time, it was deliberate. They didn't want me to know what they were saying. Maybe asking them what they were doing here was rude and none of my business.

"Well, Jim, that is two different questions," Jesus replied.

"Okay, what I mean is..."

Jesus would interrupt me. "Sorry, Jim, I know exactly what you mean. I just want you to understand what you are asking first, so when I answer your questions, we both feel you understand why we are here and what we are doing."

"Understood, and uhh understood." I tried to make a joke, but neither was laughing.

"Good. Let me ask you first. How did you feel at that school in Colorado after those events unfolded?"

Even though I asked for it, I wasn't expecting this curve ball. The Columbine school shooting I thought about why these two were there and if it had anything to do with me.

Trying to answer it the best I could, "Honestly, I was mad. Like many, I was really upset and wanted to do something about it."

"What could you have done?" Jesus asked.

"I don't know; at the time I only wanted to find satan and if I did, I wanted to do something to him, like kick his ass."

They both looked at me, and then looked at each other. Then the two of them busted out in laughter.

Pilate said, "You understand that satan probably hasn't had his ass kicked in... forever!" Again, they both laughed.

Before I could come back with a remark, Jesus looked at me and asked Pilate the question, "Το άτομο με enthousiasmos." He looked at Pilate and they both shook their head yes.

"I know that you understand nothing of ancient languages. Because of our work, it requires us the understanding of them all. Pilate and I have been far and have seen much. The language that we have been speaking is Greek. You might say Old Greek. What I asked Pilate if you were the man with the enthousiasmos. Or Enthous for short. We both agreed.

"What do you mean? I'm sorry, but I'm a little lost." I asked.

"I speak with our father often. Our Heavenly Father that is. We speak of things past, present, and the future. Our work on earth is becoming tiring. Our work is near the end. Along our path, we have been introduced to people through different means who help our mission. Many people from various backgrounds. They all have their purpose according to God's plan. In Colorado, we were introduced to a man. That man came running after us like he'd seen satan and wanted to kick his ass. Excuse my language."

We all three smirked by the way he said it. I was shocked that he used the word ass. By the way Pilate was laughing, I think it might also be the first time he'd ever heard that word from Jesus.

"Before the event in Colorado, I was told by my Father that I would meet a man one day. A man full of Enthous. That's all I was told. When I met him, I would know. This man would be necessary. This man might do for our Father what perhaps no other could. He would be good to help us with our work. We could count on him. I believe that Pilate and I agree, that man is you."

I'm not sure I wanted to know the answer, but I still needed to ask it, "What does that word mean, Enthous?"

"Its origin is from an old Greek language. Enthous has become the word enthusiasm in your English language. Do you know the word, Jim?"

Happy to answer a question correctly for once I replied with that same excitement. "I do. It means a person is excited, or happy about something or someone."

They both looked at one another and then back at me. Almost like they were either waiting for me to continue, or change my answer. For a half second, I felt a little uneasy.

"That is a correct meaning of the word. Unfortunately, not only has the word changed over time, but also the meaning from its origin. Jim, the word Enthous means 'Inspired by God'."

"Inspired by God?" I asked.

"Yes. When a man or woman has Enthous it means the work they do, the words they speak, or the actions and purpose of their daily routines are inspired by God. What they are working on, what they are involved with, the goals and plans of their life, are all inspired by God. Not all have it. Many have the desire, but not the heart or strength to persevere."

There was another brief moment of silence before Jesus continued, "You do know that some of God's gifts are burdens. Not always do they appear to be gifts, but rather tasks that

184

many cannot handle. So, back to Colorado in the spring of 1999."

Jesus had this look on his face that my father used to have. It was one of those looks when a question was asked and dad already knew the answer. I was asked a question with an answer expected. Now I just had to answer it.

"The country has seen all kinds of bad things done to innocent people before that day. But for some reason, maybe because it involved kids and the gunmen were their classmates, or maybe it was because that part of the country seemed so quiet and peaceful, it really bothered people. For me, I knew satan had to be behind it. I had already been looking for years. Looking for him when just about anything bad happened."

"Well, why did it happen?" Jesus asked.

"Well they said it was because the two students or gunmen were..."

Jesus interrupted again, "I know what was said as society tried to find blame. But Jim, what was the blame, or is there blame?"

"To be honest, all I remember hearing is these guys were outcasts. Each a hated stereotype and had anger issues or some kind of rage that they couldn't deal with."

"Ahhh... I also do remember hearing those theories from many of the experts and many leaders in your society. Many of the people in charge of the well-being of you all. Of course, each trying to find blame for an action that was not the result of something those two men were dealing with or had done wrong."

At times over the past several hours, I was lost. I was speaking with Jesus Christ and although at some point he always made sense, he was speaking over my head. Just like the Bible, each story had a purpose, and once you understood the details, everything else fell into place and made perfect sense.

"I'm a little lost, Jesus. I'm not sure anyone knew exactly why they did what they did."

Jesus perked up and sat upright in his chair. "Let me ask it in another way. What would cause those two boys to harm so many?"

"Well, luckily it was less than what it could have been. But I guess..."

Again, Jesus interrupted. "Lucky you say? You only have a guess, but truly you have no idea!"

"What do you mean?" I asked confused, but eager for a response.

"We'll get to that later. Now, any more thoughts on why those two boys would commit murder?"

"I guess rage and anger."

"All of that is true, but those feelings were the unfortunate result of something else, Something much bigger."

"Maybe some kind of abuse at home, or some kind of abuse with drugs or something?"

Both Jesus and Pilate shook their heads side to side. "You missed the same problem that has killed so many great nations. So many great people all missed the same things you are missing. History repeats itself often, and every time the end comes to those who ignore the obvious."

"I need your help to understand. Please tell me, I would like to know," I pleaded.

"It has been witnessed time and time again: the Persians, Greeks, Meads, Romans. They have all had the same disease. Scripture tells of the end having signs, many signs. One being the incurable disease. For centuries, it's been thought of as a disease of flesh and blood. But the incurable disease is that of the sin."

I said nothing as he sat there and continued. "Jim, have you ever been troubled by the decline of social moral values? The overextension of military by a country used to wage war? How about your society's acceptance and embracing of sexual immorality? The power of your government to rule and control its citizens? Or basic social unrest? Are not these the reason a couple of students go to school to harm classmates and friends?"

Well, this is what you get with Jesus. A verbal hammer. He hits you with the truth and brings things to light that have gone unnoticed. I'm not sure how to feel. It is all overwhelming. Talking with them has been unexplainably rewarding. But I hate the feeling of disappointment that washed over me in how we have all let him down. And not just once.

He continued, "I speak not of just a failure to be charitable. I speak not of your failure to tithe. I speak not of you or the many others who ask, but rarely give. The words of our Heavenly Father go neglected and unspoken more and more each day, do they not? I ask of you, do your children know of and understand the Ten Commandments? What of my commandments? I gave you two. Can you repeat them for me now?"

"I can. Love thy God, and love they neighbor like yourself."

"Very good Jim. Now I ask you, the school that your children attend, do they pray?"

"They do not. Prayer in school has been outlawed in about every school for many years," I replied almost feeling guilty.

"They do not pray, but they have classes for teaching lifestyle choices and accepting behaviors that are not acceptable to God. Does that seem odd to you? They do not allow Bibles in your schools, but prisons guardsmen claim they are the most requested book."

Before I could even reply, Jesus continued, "Do you not have laws written by those you choose to represent the common man of government? And many in that position use that ability to better themselves before that same common man? Every man and woman outside this system outnumbers those in government more than the stars. Is that not foolish for such a system to exist?"

I still sat speechless as he went on. "Your movies, I do not watch them, but know of each. They have plots that portray hate, rage, anger, and violence that I don't dare to see. Do they not teach violence as the only way to handle conflict? These shows and those people are rewarded by advertisements of companies to whom you support each day in the marketplace. Jim, you have a daughter. Would you exchange a product or service at the expense of your daughter's moral well-being? You have and continue to do so! Tell me I am wrong."

Ashamed is the word that best describes how I was feeling. Jesus continued for what seemed like forever. Not one single word, or example, or question he had was a surprise or an unknown idea. As always, he was right about it all. I'd just never heard it questioned in the manner in which he continued.

I have broken most of the ten commandments. Everyone I know has done the same. Lying, cheating, stealing, some form of adultery. These acts by man are all understood and forgiven because of Jesus' sacrifice. I believe that. I've never committed murder though. For most, committing murder is the ultimate sin, but Jesus reminded me that murder in scripture isn't the same as killing.

What is killing? It is the act of doing physical harm to someone that causes their life to stop. Or is killing the stripping of morals? Or the undoing of a system set up to protect us from doing the unthinkable? Or is it just the acceptance that life is sometimes hard and unfair and that a simple set of rules goes so un-noticed and there is acceptance that it has just become normal? After you have killed off the spirit within and the spirit around, what is left? Jesus would remind me what is left. And that is murder and how easily it comes.

"So tell me Jim, who might be to blame for the Columbine tragedy? Who should have been sued? Whom should our Father judge? Only those two students?"

I answered with the truth on my heart, "No, He should judge us all."

John
Chapter 3 Verse 16

For God so loved the world that he gave his one and only Son, that whoever believes in him shall not perish but will have eternal life.

NIV

Chapter 19

316

ON JUST ABOUT EVERY VAN HALEN ALBUM there is something unique that the band does, more so what Eddie Van Halen does. He uses guitar solos and other instrumental sounds to start one of the tracks. Some of these are song lead-ins, while others actually have their own distinct tracks. On Van Halen's first album, the song, "Running With the Devil," has an introduction instrumental using car horns. Actual car horns that are recorded and used in the opening of the song. Eddie and his band mates have done work with pianos, synthesizers, of course guitars, and once he even used a cordless drill to find an "interesting" sound.

On the album "For Unlawful Carnal Knowledge," the last song on that album, "Top of the World," is my favorite. The only instrumental on the album comes right before this track. Track number ten, has a little guitar solo named "316."

I heard a story once that 316 is a code for police to use as a street disturbance or demonstration. Sounds about right for a rock-and-roll band. The famous Whiskey-a-Go-Go nightclub in Hollywood, California has had many 316's, I'm sure, outside their doors on the nights of a Van Halen concert.

Another rumor running around is that 316 is an instrumental

about his son. A soft lullaby or guitar love story about his one and only child. The reason to call the lullaby 316? It's his son's birthday, March 16. I'm not sure which story is true, but there was one last story about what that 316 might mean. There's another man who loved the world so much he gave his one and only son as proof of that love. John 3:16.

At one point in the evening during Jesus and Pilate's visit, we discussed a few stories from the book of John. I probably could have asked about Van Halen and the 316 references, but for what purpose? Even though the guys I was sitting with probably knew it's meaning, it would have been silly and a waste of time. As the conversation moved on, I sensed that something important was coming. The tone in their voices had changed. I didn't sense anything bad, but the questions and statements they made all started heading in a general direction. Very soon one of these two were going to hit me with something. I just knew it.

This wasn't an accidental meeting and from the course of our conversation, I could see the change. It went from the fun of "good guys" having a conversation to an inquiring type of lesson. Now we are at the heavy-hearted part, "what do you think, and what are you going to do now?" They were here to visit with me, but I was the guest.

Jesus has repeatedly asked about my understanding of scripture. Each time we come to the topic he was serious and stern. We talked through many stories but mostly covered the book of John.

There's a story in the book of John about a woman who was caught in the act of sleeping with a married man. John, Chapter Eight, I believe. In today's society that type of behavior, adultery, is often ignored or maybe only scoffed at. Too often in today's modern world, adultery from either the man or woman is celebrated. Our world of cable channels and reality TV has, at times, placed a prize on what was obviously an immoral act

2,000 years ago. Rarely today is the behavior of adultery even spoken of poorly, much less punished. However, 2,000 years ago? It could carry a death sentence.

Apparently, the entire throwing stones that we all speak of in our own trials of life is a story that comes from that affair. One day way long ago, there was a group of people not necessarily believing this guy Jesus and what he was trying to sell. They believed his story was bull and needed a way to prove it. Just like today, in every group there are doubters. Well in this story, one of the citizens in the mob knew of a relationship between an unmarried woman and a married man.

Back then, laws were a little easier to understand. They weren't volumes of books with thousands of pages like we have today, but rather a basic understanding of the government and the needs of society. They also had these things called the Ten Commandments. That was about it. It's sad how we've lost sight of the simplicity in those laws.

Jesus said one person in the mob shared this secret amongst the others about the unholy and unlawful relationship. It was determined that not only would this woman be brought out amongst all for punishment, but it might be well worth doing it while this guy, Jesus, who is claiming to be the Son of Man, be present. What a better way to condemn a sinner and at the same time prove this man "Jesus" to be a fraud.

The story goes that Jesus was out and about one day and sure enough, this woman was found in bed with this married man. Quickly, people from the mob grabbed her and took her to an area where he also was. Jesus typically moved with large crowds around him, so this would be perfect for the mob's purposes. To find the largest group in town typically meant that you would find Jesus.

Right in front of him, the mob proclaimed this woman to be an adulterer and reminded Jesus that the punishment for such an act was stoning. As they continued to site to him the law of not only the land, but also the law of God, he began to write something in the sand below his feet. He said he wasn't ignoring them, but Jesus told me that he continued to write while the mob continued to yell for justice.

"What were you writing?" I asked.

"Something I do for a purpose," Jesus replied

"Huh? That doesn't make any sense."

Before Jesus could reply, Pilate would add, "It never does." He shook his head slightly while glancing at Jesus and laughed a bit.

So, I left it alone. Jesus continued about what the mob was demanding to be done. He also briefly spoke to me of the woman in this story. He spoke of her past, who she was, and what she did. Hers was life full of struggles, pain, suffering, discouragement, and illness. Hearing Jesus go on and on you could assume this woman was a wreck. Then of course Jesus hit me with this.

"She was one of my favorites. A true believer, teacher, and protector," he said.

"A protector of what?" I asked.

"To her last breath, she protected me."

The look on his face was again serious. So again, I left that one alone. Jesus continued telling the story. Groups of people came before the mob to hear what the citizens and any others involved with the situation might have to say. If enough people thought you were guilty, they stick around. The others all often leave. Either way, if you were found guilty of a crime, like adultery, then being stoned to death was often the punishment. During that day, not a single person came to defend the woman.

Jesus continued about how the mob insisted that she was guilty. Even by her own tongue she admitted to the crime. The verbal assault for justice wasn't just directed toward her. The mob wanted to see the miracle worker, Jesus Christ, save her. Scripture makes it very clear not to temp the Lord, but to temp the Son? The mob was attempting to use that day and this woman as proof that the Jesus' stories and tales of him being the Son of Man were also a lie.

As he told the story, I could see his eyes drift from my face to another time. He still stared straight at me as he continued, but you could tell he was recalling the faces of each person that day. His face and eyes were looking ahead, but his mind was looking behind. He spoke of the fear and guilt she showed. He said she begged for help. Begged to be forgiven, screaming and crying all the while. He spoke of the rage and anger in the mob's voices. But it was the hate toward her that bothered him the most. Heartbreaking, is how he described it.

Focused on me as he continued with an almost cocky tone and expression, he said. "I looked right at the mob. There were a couple men out front who were the leaders, and I spoke. I stood up and as calmly as was required for all to hear, I instructed them to stone away."

"What? How could you just..." I was beginning to ask, but he immediately cut me off.

"I told them that the law of both God and land for the sin of adultery was punishable. Yes, I do agree. However, I looked at the first man in front of me and I said this, to be understood by all who were there that day, 'Let the man who has lived without sin be the first to throw a stone.'"

Jesus sat there and stared right at me. He had the grin on his face like he had answered the million-dollar question and won the prize. Cocky wasn't the expression, but rather triumh. Pilate made a "hmm" noise, like he was approving what Jesus had done. I obviously wasn't there that day, but I could sure feel the experience. The angry mob had come to push, test, or tempt the Son of God. They didn't plan on being pushed back, or at least not like that.

"Then what happened?" I asked.

"Well, nothing. Not a word was said, nor a stone thrown. I returned to my thoughts in the sand and the mob left."

"Where did the woman go, or what became of her?"

"Like I said, she was one of my favorites. From that day forward, I asked that she sin no more. And sin again she never did. She went on to have a fulfilling, long, loving life. To her last breath, she defended me to all those who questioned my place or purpose. Her current place in our Fathers mansion is one of a kind. A gift for a faithful believer, a gift for a child of God."

Again, a pause. The two of them sat there looking at me like it was my turn to talk. I really didn't have anything to say. I'd heard bits of this story before, but I've never heard it told that way. Never told with the emotion of actually being there. I was almost drained just listening to it. Honestly, I didn't want it to end.

We sat there for another eight to ten seconds of silence before I finally spoke. "I need to be direct. Why exactly are you here with me, and what are you really doing?"

Without hesitation Jesus began to answer, "Jim, I am here for the same reason that I always have been. I save lives. Those who follow me shall know little harm, and shall meet our Heavenly Father without delay. Your grandfather down the hall will meet our Father soon!"

I started to tear up. My heart hurt hearing him say it. I knew he was going soon. But hearing Jesus say it? I felt pain.

Half a second later, I redirected our conversation, "So what about those poor kids in that school in Colorado? Or how about any of the things I've seen over the past several years? So many horrible things and places. It just pains me and makes me sick to think of the hell they went through before any of those people died."

The look on Jesus' face was almost painful. It was an expression of disgust not with the question about Columbine or one of the other events, but rather I think he was surprised at my question.

Before I could reply, he continued, "Jim, you were correct in all your journeys. The evil one had touched souls along the way.

Yeah, he's done some bad things! All those acts of violence, all the death and destruction to so many. All those places you have traveled, he'd been to them all. On his back, yes you were. Often not late by hours, but rather days, weeks and even years. Jim, he walks amongst us yes, but he is a coward. He won't be seen, not yet. Second to only my Father is his power. Know this though. He's terrified, scared, and running. Running like prey from a larger animal."

I sat there and he continued speaking about satan and his plan. Satan's plan that is. He told a few stories of events that I've never heard about. He asked me questions about my thoughts of the devil and he spoke about satan for another minute or two. He didn't speak kindly, but direct and to the point. As he continued, I asked a question that he would answer in a fashion that might trouble me for the rest of my life.

"What do you mean exactly by scared and running? Running from you two?" I asked.

They sat there again quietly for a minute. Again, they looked at one another before looking back at me. His voice was clear and direct. "No, Jim, he's not scared or running from us. He is scared and running from you."

Exodus 14:13-14

Fear not, stand firm, and see the salvation of The Lord, which He will work for you today... The Lord will fight for you, and you have only to be silent.

NIV

Chapter 20

Monday Night Football

"Now that's funny! Running and afraid of me?" I said sarcastically.

"Well yes Jim, he is. Why would that be funny?" Jesus replied.

"Oh, I don't know... satan, the "other" guy in power, afraid of me? How could that be possible?"

"Well, simple. He's a coward. He is weak and looks for weakness amongst all men. That is all. This is the very reason for our visit with you. We are here to meet you and prepare you for the coming days, months, and years ahead. Everything we believe and know of you, he knows the same. All your strengths, all of your abilities, and yes, he also understands your future. He knows all too well the meaning of Enthous. He knows exactly where it comes from. He sees it in you as well."

This is the part I have been dreading. Over the past several hours we have discussed the how, what, and why I've done things. Where I've gone and what I was thinking when I went there. For the better part of the past several hours I've had to endure my past. Unfortunately, not always the best of times were remembered. However, I had to wait for the right moment before I could ask...

"What did you mean, my future?"

Both Jesus and Pilate sat up in their chairs and looked briefly at one another. It was obvious that I had asked a question that was not going to be answered lightly, or at least they hadn't planned on answering it yet. Pilate again asked Jesus something and Jesus replied in that old language.

"Jim, was the event at that school in Colorado the most troubling for you?" Jesus asked.

"The most troubling? I'm not sure. Everywhere I've been to, looking for satan was troubling. I've not really thought about it like that before."

"Well, perhaps I will ask it in another way. In your life, what event bothers you the most? What troubles you about not only what happened, but an event that caused you to question your faith?"

"That's easy. It was September 11, 2001," I said without hesitation.

"Ah," Jesus said shaking his head.

He sat there for a moment without saying a word. I waited for a response as he had a contemplating look on his face. I could see the wheels turning in his head. His eyes got teary and his cheeks rose, bringing his lips almost to a smile. Then the shocker.

"What a great day for both of us," Jesus said while looking at Pilate.

"Excuse me? A *great* day for the two of you?" I said, slightly irritated.

Up until now, Pilate had only contributed in small doses. His comments were very deliberate and to the point. Always short and direct. Any interruptions with Jesus or myself were needed. The very second I questioned Jesus about it being a great day, Pilate looked at me like he wanted to jump down my throat.

"Yes, it was a great day," he responded immediately.

"I had the opportunity to walk so many people into our Father's home. Anytime I meet my brothers and sisters it is a great day for me. A great day, every day. Dying is only hard for those left behind, for those still living amongst us on earth. For the newly deceased (my followers) it's the beginning of something special.

He paused for a brief second and continued. Almost like he had to catch his breath, "Death to the living is so final. The end of a life is so hard for those still alive. But I ask you, are you a man of faith?"

I nodded my head quickly up and down without saying a word.

"I have asked others before, and I will ask you again now. Are you not a man of faith? Have you not proclaimed to others, both family and friends that you believe in our Father, believe in me? You have told many in your life stories about my teachings. Even through the divorce with Jennifer, you still took your children to church. What a great commitment you have made to our Father and me. Yet so many struggle with death as if it is the end. Where does your faith take you when confronted with death?"

I don't even know how to respond. I almost feel like I'm in some kind of trouble. I sat there staring at them both. They had a look of disappointment. I sat there frozen, upset with myself.

"Your grandfather is dying down the hall. Are you happy for him, or are you sad for yourself?"

Before I could even think or reflect about that statement from Jesus, Pilate jumped at the opportunity to respond.

"September 11th was a great accomplishment," he said.

Shocked and equally puzzled I asked, "How could that be a great accomplishment?"

Pilate continued, "Jim, have you ever forgotten or lost something that kept you late for an appointment or meeting because you had to return home to get it?"

"You mean, like my car keys? Of course, everyone has," I responded.

200

"What if I told you that some of those lost items or misplaced valuables that delayed you were not by accident."

Again, both Pilate and Jesus sat there looking at me. This time though, they had grins on their faces like they knew something I didn't. It was the grin on a child's face when they've been caught doing something they shouldn't have been doing.

Pilate asked, "Do you like American football, Jim?"

"Yeah, of course. I love the Kentucky Wildcats and the Dallas Cowboys."

"Ah, your home team and America's team. I understand. We, however, have no favorites. Or should I say, I didn't have a favorite until September 10, 2001. The New York Giants and the Denver Broncos drew a little more interest, more so than ever before that game has our attention."

"Okay, but why those two?" I asked.

"They played the first game that year on Monday evening, the 10th of September," Pilate said.

"Okay, but I still don't understanding."

Jesus sat still while Pilate continued, "For many years prior to that day, the first Monday of football season has an evening contest for each new season of American football, I believe you call the NFL? Traditionally, this game is between two teams and it's played in the city from the prior year's champion. The first game in 2001 should have been played in Baltimore. The home of the Ravens who won the championship in January of 2001. However, if you recall, that game was in Denver. The Broncos had not even played in the championship that year.

I had an eerie feeling come over me. Goosebumps and every hair on my body once again stood on end. Again, I just sat there and looked at both men, waiting for them to go on. They still had the same serious grin on their faces. They were grinning about the little secret that I was about to be let in on.

Pilate continued. This time though, the grin disappeared. His voice was more serious, and he spoke very clearly. He wanted to me pay attention. "Through scripture you should know that God makes it known that no man, including his own son sitting here, can mettle with free will. The free will of each man and woman alive was given to each soul born as a gift. As bad as intended actions may be, and although we may know the plans, we cannot stop them."

I interrupted, "That's sad. You know about the plans of these nut jobs out there and you cannot stop them? Several thousand people died, and we just chalk it up to free will?"

Just as soon as I ended my statement, Jesus spoke out positively, "Fortunately for many though, that game was played in Denver."

It became obvious and I had to ask, "Did you guys have something to do with that? Did you guys make that game happen in Denver?"

They looked at each other before refocusing on me. Pilate said something to Jesus in their language again. I'm guessing he was asking permission to say something secret. Jesus then turned his head towards Pilate then again towards me and answered him in English so I could understand.

"We can trust him," he said.

Pilate nodded like he was receiving instructions and then continued, "Yes, Jim, for many years the host city for the first Monday night football game in your country has been held in the prior season's champion's city. Well, that year, the game was held in Denver, Colorado. We knew of the horrible events that were going to unfold that day. The 11th day of September in 2001. We had known for many years."

What I heard next almost made me sick to my stomach.

"It was like when your grandfather went on leave from the Navy before the birth of your aunt."

There was that grin again.

"Why would that have anything to do with September 11th?" I asked, confused.

"Those events directly? Nothing. The Japanese nation chose to attack the United States for various reasons. People were going to die. We were going to lose many great people. Fathers, sons, uncles, brothers, and plenty of great women as well. However, there were several people we couldn't lose. Your grandfather was one of them. I actually saved his tail a few times. I believe you know that was me in the picture of your grandfather's crew in the Navy.

"Yeah! That's right, I remember. My little brother pointed you out while they were looking through the photo album," I said excitedly.

"Yes, that was me," he said with a smile, "As I said, we needed your grandfather alive. If he had died, then your mother would not have been born. You would have not been born."

"Why me? Why would you need me alive so badly?" I said.

Jesus answered my question with a head nod and a smile, "Not for anything you have done, but for what you are going to do."

That statement sounded both frightening and exciting at the same time. What I was going to do? I didn't ask what because that would be like asking about when I would die or something. I didn't want to know. Quickly I had to redirect the conversation.

"Okay, but what was going on with the football game?"

Pilate answered, "Well, as I was saying, for years that day, September 11 had been in the works. We understood the conditions and the circumstances. We knew it all, but we couldn't stop the will of any man. We could only take steps to alter the outcome. We had a chance to save lives that day and it took us several years to prepare for it."

I couldn't wait for him to continue.

"The New York towers, at the time of the attacks, on a normal day would have had double, if not triple, the number of people in them. Because that game was played in Denver, the entire pace that Tuesday morning in New York was diminished. It wasn't a normal start to a Tuesday in New York. Many people had stayed home late or had that Tuesday morning off because of that game. We couldn't save everyone, but we were able to protect a large number of people. Denver had just built a new stadium and that Monday was the first game held there. The offices of the league government, again, you call it the NFL, had promised the ownership of the Denver football team that first game to be held in the new stadium would be the first Monday game of the season. Before they built it, Denver residents had to approve the extra taxes. I'll spare you the details, but I'm sure you can put together how long prior to September of 2001 we were working to ensure all these events took place."

He continued for another few minutes about the process and how they could reduce the death toll in one city by an event happening in another. In this case, they were talking about thousands of people. In my case, it was a single life. Apparently it has been done many times before, whether for one life or for many. If I was needed alive, my grandfather would also have to survive. These two obviously meddled in ways we don't understand for the purpose of completing a bigger plan.

Maybe it wasn't luck that kept Gramps alive during WWII, but rather a guy named Pilate. For whatever reason, they wanted me born so he had to be protected. Why? I haven't got a clue, nor am I sure if I want to know. I did feel like I needed to ask one more question.

"Jesus, will my grandfather be alright?"

Jesus replied with a bright face and a sincere smile. Shaking his head yes, "Jim, your grandfather is in great hands."

Almost relieved, I sat back and relaxed. But right then, Jesus hit me with what I was afraid of.

His smile started to fade, "However, your grandfather will pass within the hour."

1 Corinthians
Chapter 2 Verse 9

What no eye has seen, nor ear heard,
nor the heart of man imagined, what God has
prepared for those who love him.

NIV

Chapter 21

Moments Matter

6:38 p.m.

GRAMPS HAD A STROKE during that fishing trip in Taylorsville in late August of 2006. The fishing trip I never made it to. He had been out in the heat and humidity all morning and a little after lunch time, he collapsed. Right about the same time I should have shown up. I was out chasing after satan when I should have been fishing with Gramps. I thank God every day that he didn't die that afternoon. If he had died, I would have never forgiven myself.

Following his stroke, for several months, times were tough on me but, even more, it was hell for Gramps. The stroke had left permanent damage. Talking and walking wasn't automatic for him anymore. Although he had the mental capacity to do both, the muscle reaction from his brain needed to be relearned for the left side of his body.

That process took seven days a week for months. Luckily for us, we live around Fort Knox. The base there had some incredible First Responders. And lucky for Gramps he was a veteran. A Vet of WWII, no less. They all loved him there.

I couldn't make it happen every day, but whenever possible,

I did everything I could to get him to and from the hospital. He didn't have the energy of a young man. He was, after all, in his late 70s.

The whole hospital process was brutal and mentally draining, but also a physical challenge. Every day was a solid six to eight hours with this nurse or that specialist for gramps. Seeing Gramps in that condition and fighting to relearn how to walk was tough on my spirits, much less his.

I learned quickly a few things about going through something like this with a loved one. First, the average nurse is a miracle worker. That is no lie. Most are a blessing and a true gift from God. Ours were the absolute best. I also learned about living with less and still being happy. Each day is a gift. Just because our normal daily activities ceased, didn't mean we didn't still have everything. After all, we still had one another. I knew then and struggled with the reality that Gramps and I would never fish again after his stroke. I missed out on our last fishing trip together. I'll never fish again without being reminded of gramps.

I also learned about grace. Needing, without having a thing to give, can humble just about anyone. I was worried about my dignity, and Gramps was always a proud man, so seeing him struggle with bodily care meant that I had to suck it up, too.

The most important thing I learned during this ordeal was about love. I love my children more than anything. At one time in my life, Jennifer was more important to me than anyone, but that eventually passed. My parents have been gone for longer than I knew them alive. I miss them and loved them the best way I could. But I never knew about love until sitting there with Jesus. And with my best friend dying just down the hallway, it was starting to sink in how much I truly loved him.

"I am sorry Jim, but he will pass within the hour," Jesus said again.

And without a word from anyone, Jesus asked, "And how does this make you feel?"

"Sad. I understand that dying is a part of life, and he has had a great life. But still, I will miss him."

The three of us sat there. For a moment I didn't have anything to say. The last several hours, although unbelievably rewarding, had been exhausting. We sat for a few minutes without a word until I finally spoke.

"Jesus, Pilate, I want to say thank you. Although I would rather not be here under the circumstances, I appreciate the past several hours. And as much as I want to stay and talk to you, I need to go spend my grandfather's last hour with him. I'm sorry, but I need to leave."

"You have got nothing to be sorry about," Jesus said with a smile.

And at almost the same time, Pilate included, "We have hope for you."

I stood up and prepared to leave the lobby and head towards Gramps' side. I stopped for a second while standing and looked at both of them straight in the eyes. I wanted them to know exactly how serious I was.

"Thank you, Pilate. I'm glad to hear that. It makes me feel good, really good. But understand this. You called it Enthous, Inspired by God? Is that correct?"

Without a word spoken, they both nodded their head as to say yes.

"That's just about right. I do feel inspired by God. I'll never quit. This morning I knew I was looking for satan. That was a mistake. This evening I know I've been looking for something or someone else. What exactly? I'm not sure. But I promise both of you I'll never quit."

"I know that, Jim. We are going to need you. More than you can possibly imagine," Jesus responded.

I really didn't know what he was referring to. To tell you the truth though, I didn't care. If I've ever known one thing, it's this ride in life that we are on is God's plan, not ours. If they needed me for something, so be it. I gave them one last friendly wave as I turned to walk down the hall.

"Funny, Jim." Pilate spoke out.

"What's that?" I blurted out as I stopped and turned my head back around.

I stepped back toward them.

"In all my travels around the world, we have many times had similar run-ins with people throughout the centuries. And again, you are the first."

"Again?" I asked.

"Yeah, the first who actually tracked us down, and now this!"

"What's that?" I asked them both, truly unknowing of what he was referencing.

"Don't you need some kind of proof? Something that you can trust or believe in by something other than our words today?"

"Nope. I have all the proof I need."

Both of them sat there waiting for me to continue, waiting for what was coming next.

"Fellas...It's called faith!"

All three of us bust out giggling. I didn't plan for it to come out as funny, but it just did. I'm not sure why either, but it was how I felt. If these two were not who they claimed to be, then I was the fool. However, my heart just knew. And again, as I was turning around and waving goodbye, Jesus hit me with another shocker.

"Jim, I do want to give you a gift, but I would like to know what you want."

"Like what? The lotto numbers?" I don't think Jesus found that funny, but he did respond.

"If that's what you'd like, I can make that that happen," he said with an authoritative voice.

I stood there for a minute without responding. I didn't want the lotto numbers. That was just me being a smart ass. He knew it, too. When Gramps and I played poker he always told me to never bluff someone smarter than me. Jesus called my bluff, but if I could ask for a gift, what to ask for?

Eternal life? Sounds tiring. All knowing knowledge? Sounds painful. To end world hunger? Bring peace to the planet? Both of those seemed too large. What could I possibly ask for from Jesus that would serve myself and others around me? I had a feeling he wanted to give me something that I perhaps needed, and only needed to ask.

Then from nowhere, it hit me. I knew exactly what I wanted. "I would like five minutes. Five minutes with my grandfather as he was when he was at his best. Physically strong and mentally healthy. I would like to go into his room and talk with him and yes, say goodbye. Just five minutes before you take him. That's all I would like."

Jesus shook his head a tad and with the glowing smile said, "Jim, you continue to impress and make me proud. You don't have five minutes, however. You've got ten. I know both of you will enjoy it."

Without a second more wasted, I turned around and began the walk down the hallway. My grandfather was 83 years old. This was his second stroke. Rehabilitation and a reduced physical state had taken their tolls. As I walked down the hall, I didn't think for a second about the men behind me. I was only thinking about the man in front of me.

His room was directly across the nurse's station. Room number 229. There was a good amount of activity coming from other rooms. Both from medical staff and visiting friends and families. As I walked closer, I was both excited and fearing what I was walking into. Earlier, gramps lay there unresponsive. He couldn't respond to anything I asked or said. As I sat with him earlier that day, I had no idea if he could hear a word I said.

The closer I walked toward his room, the more anxious I became. If he was up and alert, what were we going to talk about? If he was alert, I'm not saying goodbye for the day, I'm saying goodbye forever. The closer I got to the door, the tougher this was becoming. I did take comfort in one thing, however. As I rounded the corner of the door, I knew that if he wasn't alert, the two guys in the waiting area were nothing more than con men. At minimum, I'd at least have that.

We made eye contact immediately and without hesitation Gramps yelped out with this booming voice, "Jimmy!" I think he was more excited about seeing me than I was of him. He was speaking with his old voice that I hadn't heard in years. Gramps always had a very heavy sound, full of southern twang, and always full of life. He had lost it years ago after his first stroke. He hadn't sounded this spirited in years.

As I grabbed the chair and sat next to his bed, I had not a clue what we were going to talk about. What I was going to say? How I was going to say goodbye? I asked Jesus for five minutes and he gave me ten. Ten minutes was a blessing, but now what?

He spoke first before I could get a word out. "Jimmy, did you hear the one about the grandmother's family trip to Israel?" Gramps had a joke or a story about everything. I remember him most for all his jokes. He told jokes to everyone, and I mean everyone. And he had jokes about everything. Most were rated PG, though some a little closer to rated R. Every one of them though was a story.

"So Jimmy, there's this family from Chicago that had this granny who wanted to see her homeland in Israel. She was an old lady, who was close to the end. Her last wish was a trip to Israel with the entire family. Kids, grand kids, brothers, sisters, everyone. It took years, but in her early 90s, her dream was coming true.

"The husband of her oldest daughter put in all the work. He planned the entire trip. It was a two-week journey and Granny couldn't wait.

"Halfway through the trip, at a time when the family was

having a ball, Granny passed away while sleeping. Although unexpected, the family all took comfort in the fact that this was the perfect end to her life."

As Gramps told the joke, I noticed the clock on the nightstand... we had eight minutes left together.

Gramps continued, "The family still had another six days in Israel. Now they had to plan not only a funeral back in the USA, but to fly her body back as well. The same son-in-law who planned the trip also took on that responsibility. He found a company that could handle everything, but it would cost five grand to care for her body and fly her home. At the same time, arrangements were being made back in Chicago that would cost another ten grand. They had dates for the funeral and families and friends began planning the day for when they arrived back in Chicago. But then, a rumor from one of the hotel's workers surfaced while they were still in Israel.

"Apparently, there were grave sites and services right there in Israel where they graciously buried anyone who loved Jesus Christ. The entire process was immediate, very professional, personal, and with that special touch of Christian flare that Granny would absolutely love. The entire process would only cost $500.

"Once the son-in-law heard the news he made it very clear, 'No way are we burying Granny here. She's going back to Chicago, period!'

"Granny's daughter and her husband went round and round. Most everyone in the family couldn't believe his proclamation. Everyone shared their thoughts on the issue and pleaded with the man to reverse his decision. Nobody could understand the sense in spending all that money, time, and effort while all the while the funeral could be done tomorrow for 500 bucks.

"The daughter of the grandma pleaded with her husband in front of the entire group, 'Please, hun, let's just do this and be done.' He still stood firm and shook his head no.

"She asked, 'But why, hun, why?'

"His reply: 'Sweetheart, please understand. I know this has been a great trip for everyone. I know how much it meant to your mother. Yes, it is a whole lot more money to fly her home and bury her there. I understand how easy it would be to have it all done tomorrow. But understand this. I don't know a lot about these parts, but I once heard about a fella named Jesus who died, was buried, and came back to life three days later. Now sweetheart, I just can't take the chance that the same thing might happen with your mother!'"

Seven minutes left.

We both had a good chuckle. I'm not sure when it happens, but there is one thing I notice about senior citizens. Sometime later in life, they all develop this little angle in the corner of their eyes. It looks like a squint, but up close it's actually a sparkle. I sat right there giggling at that joke and both the corners of his eyes had that joyful sparkle.

Gramps continued the small talk. We spoke about Jen, his grandkids, and my brothers. He asked me how I thought the Cowboys were going to do this year. As he continued to talk, I struggled to find things I wanted to say.

Don't get me wrong, I wanted to talk forever, but the clock was ticking. Literally ticking away. Jesus had blessed me with ten minutes. I wanted to talk about everything, but in my head I knew some things I didn't want to waste time on. But what should I talk about? What would be the best way to spend my last few minutes with Gramps?

Five minutes left.

As great as this gift was, it was also equally painful. The more I thought about this entire thing, the more I had to fight back emotions that I wasn't ready to share. I knew he would be gone in minutes. I watched my parents die in that horrible accident years ago, but at least it was unexpected and by surprise. This time, death was coming, and I knew when. The more the clock ticked the more uncomfortable I became.

Gramps seamed completely at peace. He was comfortable and continued to go on about everything. He could bounce around from sports to the weather to politics like it was all weaved together. Oddly, it always was. His nature was pleasant. His interest was always in the other person's pleasure. He spoke more about nonsense than any man I ever knew, but sitting right there it dawned on me. His rambling wasn't nonsense, but rather perfect sense. He made perfect sense about everything, I just hadn't always listened.

He often told me that listening isn't the same as hearing. He'd say you can hear all day long and not understand a darn thing. He'd tell me and my little brothers that the good Lord gave us one mouth and two ears for a reason. He always encouraged us to listen more than we talk. How true that is.

Three minutes left.

As he continued to talk, I thought about asking him where he had been? Hours ago, before I meet Jesus and Pilate down the hall, he wasn't like this. Although alive, he was unresponsive. He couldn't react to anything I said, and now this? The complete opposite. He continued to jabber along like he also knew time was running out.

Two minutes left.

I found a spot mid-sentence to ask a question. I hadn't said more than a few words since entering the room. This might be it. My last opportunity. Of all things I wanted to talk about or ask, I really only had one. "Is there anything I can do for you Gramps?"

He paused and looked at me with a slightly odd look on his face. He took a deep breath and pursed his lips together like he was considering how to respond. "Yeah, there is," he said.

I sat there waiting completely motionless and careful not to interrupt. He looked me square in the eyes and before he uttered a word his eyes shifted toward the door. Maybe he heard something. I heard nothing, but when I turned my head I noticed the shadow first. The shadow of two men walking in through the

214

door. Both Jesus and Pilate had made their way into the room. Nobody said a word.

Our last minute together.

As I turned my head and attention back toward gramps, his eyes were already fixed on me. It was that smile that I will remember forever, my last memory perhaps. He still hadn't responded to my question and I couldn't fight the tears back anymore. Although I didn't make a sound, tears from both eyes starting flowing like open faucets.

"Yes Junior, I'd like one last favor. It might take you some time, but I need something from you."

Right then I'd have done just about anything. Anything he wanted I would have given him. I shook my head yes, "Yeah Gramps, whatever, just ask!" I replied with conviction.

"Take my grandkids fishing more."

I sat there for a second, stunned at the random request. Of all the things a man could ask for on his death bed and this is what he wanted? This wasn't even for him.

"Sure, Gramps. I will. I would love to. But why fishing?"

Again, he smiled and just a split second before responding he looked toward Jesus, then back toward me. His reply to my question? "Cause Jesus loves fisherman!"

I squeezed his hand without a word. Again, I shook my head yes without a word. Tears flowing. This of course made perfect sense. Is there anything better in the world than time with your kids fishing?

He blinked once and when his eyes re-opened, the color was gone. His blue eyes were now gray. At the same time, his hand went limp. He had stopped breathing. I looked again over my shoulder towards where Jesus and Pilate were. Neither of them was standing in the room. All three of them, Jesus, Pilate, and Gramps were gone.

I spent another few minutes with him. Praying to God. Thanking God for this last ten minutes. Thanking God for all my fathers. My dad, Gramps, and himself. I thanked him for letting me be a father and the gift of my two children. But most of all, I thanked God for his own son, Jesus Christ.

I kissed Gramps on the forehead, said my final goodbye, and left the room. I didn't say a word to anyone on the way out. It was a little past eight at night. As I walked out to my truck, I stopped by a pay phone and made a couple of quick phone calls before heading home.

Jeremiah
Chapter 29 Verse 11

For I know the plans I have for you," declares the LORD,
"plans to prosper you and not to harm you, plans
to give you hope and a future.

NIV

Chapter 22

Satan's Garage Sale

THE EDUCATION SYSTEM IN THIS COUNTRY, no matter the level, requires hours of school per week. Some for only weeks at a time, others for years on end. Some of that schooling costs tens of thousands of dollars a year. We learn about math, art, science, all kinds of things. We pay for classes on how to teach classes. We take classes on how cook, drive a car, fly a plane, or bust a 2x4 in karate class.

Learning about God and his son, Jesus? That costs nothing. Not a single dime. Anyone can do it in an hour or two on any Sunday, even some Saturdays. God forbid we miss history class on Tuesday, but church on Sunday? "Ah, I think I will sleep in. Or we've got something better to do." I haven't spent the first part of my life always knowing what I've really needed, but after the past 24 hours, I know how I'll be spending my second half.

I can't recall more than a couple stories that I heard in church while growing up. Most were similar. Jesus did this, Jesus did that. If it wasn't about Jesus, something about Peter, Paul, Noah or Job seams to ring a bell. Not many stuck in my head like I wished they had. I was an average teenager who fought with their parents and grandparents every Sunday morning when talk of going to church came up.

One story I did hear while growing up, that has stuck with me, was about satan's garage sale. In this story, seems like satan is always wheeling and dealing. Picture a fast-talking used car salesman perhaps.

Every once in a while, he will have so many good deals on "stuff" that he needs to get to as many people as possible through a garage sale. Obviously, it was expressed during church that day, how long those lines could be. The story goes on that satan has all kinds of goods and various products for just about anyone. In his garage sale one Saturday morning, satan had on display some tools. Everyone who visited the garage sale noticed them and at some point, each guest checked out the tools on display at the table.

They were complicated looking tools. Each was large, some shiny, and most made of durable materials. They appeared to be good tools, all of them made to last. Each one was labeled with a tag. One side was a word and the other side was a price. One tag read murder, another read hate. The tags read all kinds of things: adultery, strife, anger, deception, envy, greed, and more. Whatever tool you were looking for, satan seemed to have just the one for you.

There was this one tool that seemed to get more attention than the others even though it was the smallest of the bunch. It was neither shiny nor durable and was the oldest looking tool of them all. It was sitting off to the side, but still drew lots of interest from satan's shoppers. Oddly, its price was more than any other tools in satan's display.

One of the shoppers happened to ask satan why that old tool was so expensive. Satan replied laughing, "That tool is called the tool of Discouragement. Not all the tools here are for everyone. But that tool, that's a great one. I use it on everyone."

In 2 Corinthians 4:8-10 it says, "We are troubled on every

side, yet not distressed; we are perplexed, but not in despair; persecuted, but not forsaken; cast down, but not destroyed."

In other words, discouragement may come in occasionally, but it should not be permanent. Nor should it be final. As long as we keep our focus on Jesus Christ and continue to get up each time we are knocked down, then every one of us will overcome and conquer.

I've thought of this story many times over the past several years. When Jen and I were struggling with our marriage, I knew who was behind it, or better yet, I knew what tool satan was using. When I've struggled in life, I've never thought about anything other than satan and his favorite tool being busy at work. And as far as my journeys around the country, well, I'll just chalk them up to successful failures.

My mother once told me something that also relates. If the devil can't make you lazy, he will make sure to keep you busy. I can't tell you how busy I've been the last several years while the important things in my life went to hell. I understand that now. I can't change the past, but perhaps I need to re-focus on what really matters in life.

I never thought I'd actually run into Jesus. I was always prepared to meet satan. But to actually meet Jesus and Pilate? Not in a million years. Sitting here thinking back, satan has been hard at work. I thought from that very first trip that he didn't want me tracking him down. But the fact is, "he" was the roadblock to many of those journeys. "He" knew I wasn't on his tail, but rather on the tail of Jesus Christ and his traveling companion, Pilate. The only tool he could use on me was discouragement.

I've spent the better part of my life searching for satan. I've searched all over the country. I have put myself, my family, my marriage, finances, and health on hold chasing a "thing" that won't be found. That won't be found unless some idiot, namely *me*, goes looking for "him." I take comfort in the fact that perhaps my pursuit was for the wrong man, and in actuality, it was for the right man. I never gave up. Enthous as Jesus called it? Inspired by God? It's probably safe to say that God planned on me running into his son. I'll believe that for the rest of my life.

***

I SAID MY FINAL GOODBYE TO GRAMPS and have been sitting in my truck for more than an hour. I will forever carry that moment. Gramps and me his last ten minutes, and the four of us that last minute. I will carry the gift that Jesus gave me into eternity. He didn't walk on water, nor did he turn water into wine. I got the gift of ten minus with Gramps to say goodbye. The only word that comes to mind right now is peace. I truly feel happy.

Sitting there, I was exhausted. I'd had a trying 24 hours. Just yesterday, I was still looking for satan, I'd received word that my grandfather was at his end, and met not only Pilate, but Jesus Christ himself. Driving home, one thing kept creeping back into my head. I can't help but think of what exactly Jesus meant when he mentioned, "My turn to help was coming." I wonder.

I reached the first stop sign out of the parking lot. Already while looking both left and right, I wasn't just looking for cars. I was looking for them. For the rest of my days, I'll be looking everywhere. I won't spend another day or dollar driving around looking at death and destruction. I truly believe and now fully understand that Jesus has that in control.

Pulling away from the stop sign I turned on the radio. Whatever channel I had left it on had the disk jockey and an on-air person who called in to the radio. They were already into their conversation when I tuned in. They were talking about missed hits, or songs that should have been hits or something or another. Just before I turned the station, something caught my ear. I listened a little more to verify the band they were talking about. After only another few seconds I heard the bands' name again. That's what I thought the caller said, Van Halen.

"So you're telling me that you think Van Halen has more classic songs that should have been hits as compared to what they already have?" said the disk jockey.

"And you don't?" said the caller, questioning in a voice of concern.

"No, no, I agree with you. There are several tracks from a few of their albums that I know in another time and day would have been top ten hits," said the disk jockey.

"Doesn't even matter who the lead singer is or what decade they are from. There is plenty of great stuff that some of your listeners have never even heard."

"I couldn't agree with you more."

"Hey," said the disk jockey "how about you pick an album, and I'll pick the song. I'll pick something nobody will see coming. How does that sound?"

"Awesome, I know exactly what album," said the caller.

"Hit me with it," the DJ replied.

"Play something off the album 'For Unlawful Carnal Knowledge.'"

"Great album. Thanks for the call," said the DJ.

The DJ continued, "Well, for all you listeners out there, enjoy this one! Off of Van Halen's 1991 album 'For Unlawful Carnal Knowledge...'"

The minute I heard the caller say the album's name and before the DJ even said the track number he was selecting, I knew exactly what song he was going to play.

"Off of Van Halen's 1991 album 'For Unlawful Carnal Knowledge,' It's a pleasure to play for you track two...Judgment Day!"

On Top of the World

...Author's Note

FIRST AND FOREMOST, I am a devout believer in God and his Son Jesus Christ. Thank you, God, for everything, especially for the gift of your Son. All things that are impossible with man, are possible with God. (Luke18:27) And yeah, I believe when we think God isn't listening, it's because his Son is right around the corner and he's on it!

As I wrote this story, I used real events to build a fictional story. While writing, sharing ideas and discussing thoughts with a friend and another person (whom I'll leave nameless) that person asked, "If God is real, how could He allow such horrible things to happen?" As we discussed it and went round and round, we agreed to disagree. I stood my ground; he stood his. Ultimately, not I nor anyone else can actually answer that question, but I do have a great idea.

That idea started over nine years ago on an airplane. I wrote an outline for the story you just read. I hope you enjoyed it. During the seven years it took to write this book, I used several computers. I did more writing, re-writing, editing, updating, and research than I could possibly put into words. At times I wrote every day. Sometimes for only a few minutes, other times for hours on end. There were periods of time where, I didn't touch the project for an entire month. It's been both a rewarding and sometimes a painful process throughout the entire seven years. The publishing process? I'll spare you those details...lol.

My name is Shawn Sandt. I was born in Kentucky, but Mom and Dad moved me to Colorado while I was still in diapers. Other than one summer in Phoenix, I've lived somewhere in Colorado ever since. I have been married, I have two kids, two brothers, and yes, my parents are alive and well.

Each of the characters in the book are fictitious. The names though, are all real. The real Jim Thompson is my longest known friend. He or I will have the unfortunate task of carrying the other man's casket to the grave. Every character in the book was named after someone I like, respect, and flat out love. Thank you all.

The events in the book used to tell a story were beyond painful to experience, much less read and do research on. The events of Columbine (being close to home) was the first thing I wanted to place in the book. Out of respect perhaps, but I don't really know why. It just worked for the book. Most people reading this, know exactly where they were when they heard the news unfolding out of Littleton, Colorado that day. Waco was a sickening event. Katrina was unfathomable, and 9/11 was well...what is understood doesn't need to be discussed. In short, pain and suffering have been part of life throughout history. One of my hopes for those who have lost someone, is know this: The end wasn't painful, they love you, think about you a ton, and that your loved one is in a better place. A WAY better place.

The idea for this book was that when we lose someone close, Jesus has them with Him minutes before the devil knows their body has died. I can't imagine, and don't believe, the final moments of one's life is anything but peace. The body might be done, but the spirit is just coming alive. I have many reasons to believe that. I know not everyone does. For those who share the same idea or something close to it, hold on to that idea. It might just help one day down the road as proof is on the way.

I'm not done with Jim yet. The second and final book in the series is well underway. I can promise a couple things. Book number two is a little darker, has an amazing ending, and that book will NOT take seven years to complete.

It is important to tell you something about me and this book. In the 9th grade, I was tested as having a 3rd grade reading level. Most wouldn't know it, but I was having some issues in school. In math, I could add faster than anyone, but I really had issues with reading and writing. I was one of those kids who used social skills to overcome my struggles with class work. I'd have to BS my way through anything that involved reading or writing. I used poor penmanship and turned in sloppy writing to mask the fact I couldn't spell or punctuate. I learned early on if my teacher could follow the story or explanation for the exercise, they probably wouldn't "mark down" for poor spelling. Why? Because they couldn't read it. I can't tell you how many times a teacher, even in college would reduce my grade because of poor penmanship, but they themselves didn't catch words here and there that were mis-spelled. Except for one professor, that is.

I was a sociology major in college. Lots of writing...lol. I actually took a typing class and did all my own typing, when required. As you may have guessed, using poor penmanship to cover up spelling and punctuation creates a different problem when you type it. I had a creative writing class in college one semester. I can't remember the paper's content, but I do remember the grade. For all of my hard work on that exercise, I earned a seven. That's seven out of a hundred. I don't even think that would constitute an F-. ???

To celebrate the work of art, I used a steak knife to hang the paper to the wall of my apartment. I actually stabbed it right to the wall. My roommate and I threw a party that weekend. Why not share the Pulitzer Prize winning paper with all our friends to enjoy? It was so bad, we cried laughing while watching people I didn't even know read it that night. Half the enjoyment was watching them struggling through it. It was beyond awful. My friends marveled that not only was I celebrating the paper, but unlike most there that night, just a few knew I started that paper only two hours prior to it being due. I BS'd my way through 12 pages having done zero research on the topic. The fact that I actually turned something in was a feat in itself. A seven though? I never could figure out that scoring system; how do you score someone a seven?

I have some parting advice I'd like to give. Anyone out there who doesn't likes reading, watch out. Readers are leaders. I was once told to never trust a guy with a TV larger than a bookcase. If you happen to be one of those people who struggle, read the prior two sentences again, and make your own decision. Reading is a door that will open things in your life that many other items you are looking for will not.

Also, to all you aspiring writers out there. Every year almost a half-million new compositions are put into print. What are you waiting for? Your true story or fantasy could change a life. As I mentioned, this project was exactly that, a project. But worth every single minute. Enjoy the experience and just write. Mechanics, punctuation, and spelling...Ahhh, that's what the right editor is for. I can't wait to read your work sometime soon.

Today, two ladies get most the credit. Kelley Kolin and Kelsey Botkin have done the leg work. I typed every page, came up with the entire story, but those two did the rest. I can't tell you what their input has meant to this project. Aldo Gurmendi, Jordan Sandt, Corrie Beth, Carl Kisner, Patrick Sandt, Annie Filce, Kendra Stewart, Stacie Velehradsky and Susie McKenzie. Thank you all for your support and contributions. There is another group, too many to list, your encouragement has meant more than you'll ever know. Thank you all. I also would like to thank the group responsible for helping the final leg of the publishing process. Jan and Joe McDaniel with BookCrafters. You have all meant the world to me.

For the past decade or so, I've attended two churches. Southeast Christian in Parker, Colorado, and Flatirons Community in Denver, Colorado. Thanks for the inspiration and love from you all.

Speaking of love, Van Halen (yeah, actually my favorite group) was a big part of this. While putting together the story, I imagined particular songs from bands I'd use on a soundtrack for a movie. After a few attempts to contact Mr. Eastwood to bring this story to the big screen, I gave up on that dream. Maybe one day, but not now. I've not met the Van Halens, yet, but they write a lot of songs about a similar topic that the good book also speaks highly of. Love.

Love all that you do. Love all those in your life. Love everything and everybody who crosses your path. Thanks for sharing my story.

Love,
Shawn